P9-CDV-041

DATE DUE

~~MAY 5 2000~~	
~~ill 4032666~~	
~~QWE 3-8-02~~	

DEMCO, INC. 38-2931

OCCASIONAL PAPER 147

Aging Populations and Public Pension Schemes

By Sheetal K. Chand and Albert Jaeger

with a Staff Team from the Fiscal Affairs Department

ST. JOSEPH'S UNIVERSITY

3 9353 00282 5980

HD
7105.3
-C48
1996

INTERNATIONAL MONETARY FUND
Washington DC
December 1996

© 1996 International Monetary Fund

Library of Congress Cataloging-in-Publication Data

Chand, Sheetal K.
    Aging populations and public pension schemes / by Sheetal K. Chand
and Albert Jaeger with a staff team from the Fiscal Affairs Department.
        p.   cm. — (Occasional paper, ISSN 0251-6365 ; 147)
        Includes bibliographical references (p.)
        ISBN 1-55775-620-1
      1. Old age pensions.   2. Aged — Economic conditions.   3. Population
forecasting.   I. Jaeger, Albert.   II. International Monetary Fund. Fiscal
Affairs Dept.   III. Title.   IV. Series: Occasional paper (International
Monetary Fund) ; no.147.
    HD7105.3.C48   1996
    332.25'2—dc21   96-47997
                                                                        CIP

Price: US$15.00
(US$12.00 to full-time faculty members and
students at universities and colleges)

Please send orders to:
International Monetary Fund, Publication Services
700 19th Street, N.W., Washington, D.C. 20431, U.S.A.
Tel.: (202) 623-7430   Telefax: (202) 623-7201
Internet: publications@imf.org

recycled paper

Contents

Tables

Charts

The following symbols have been used throughout this paper:

. . .   to indicate that data are not available;

—   to indicate that the figure is zero or less than half the final digit shown, or that the item does not exist;

–   between years or months (e.g., 1991–92 or January–June) to indicate the years or months covered, including the beginning and ending years or months;

/   between years (e.g., 1991/92) to indicate a crop or fiscal (financial) year.

"Billion" means a thousand million.

Minor discrepancies between constituent figures and totals are due to rounding.

The term "country," as used in this paper, does not in all cases refer to a territorial entity that is a state as understood by international law and practice; the term also covers some territorial entities that are not states, but for which statistical data are maintained and provided internationally on a separate and independent basis.

Preface

This study was prepared in the Fiscal Affairs Department of the International Monetary Fund by Sheetal K. Chand, Chief, Fiscal Analysis Division, in collaboration with Albert Jaeger. The study draws on a number of papers on the public pension systems in the major industrial countries, prepared by a staff team from the Fiscal Affairs Department including Frederick Ribe, Etienne de Callatay, Marco Annunziata, and Domenico Fanizza. Useful comments and advice were received from Lans Bovenberg, Daniele Franco, and Estelle James, and from many colleagues at the Fund, in particular from Peter Heller, Liam Ebrill, and Steven Symansky. The authors wish to thank Amina Elmi for research assistance, Diana Ellyn and Beulah David for secretarial aid, and Yvonne Liem for help on the bibliography. David Driscoll of the External Relations Department edited the study for publication and coordinated its production.

The study was originally prepared for a seminar of the Executive Board of the Fund. In the seminar, Executive Directors expressed a wide range of views with regard to the appropriate approach to pension reform and the pertinence of the analysis and recommendations presented in this study. The present version reflects comments and suggestions made by a number of Executive Directors. However, the study should be taken as expressing solely the views of the authors and not those of the Executive Directors or the Fund.

1 Introduction and Summary

An aging society is characterized by a growing proportion of the retired to the active working population. Societies age either when fertility rates decline so that fewer children are born, or when longevity increases, or both. Aging affects virtually all societies today, but more so the industrial countries, which have generally experienced it over a longer period and for which further pronounced aging is projected over the next four decades, at the end of which a peak in the proportion of the elderly is likely to be attained. Concerns about the challenges posed by aging populations have moved to the forefront of the public policy debate in many countries. This paper attempts to respond to some of these concerns, focusing in particular on the fiscal sustainability of public pension schemes in industrial countries.

In the industrial countries, public schemes for providing for the retired are predominantly of a pay-as-you-go (PAYG) type, whose coverage is typically comprehensive, but which are frequently supplemented by funded schemes, mostly operated by the private sector. A standard PAYG system levies payroll taxes on the working population, while paying benefits to the retired, but usually without the close person-based relationship between individual contributions and benefits that characterizes fully funded schemes. In the early stages of a PAYG system, low contribution rates are sufficient to cover benefits of a relatively small number of beneficiaries, but as the scheme matures, benefits paid out tend to exceed contributions, requiring increases in payroll taxes or budget transfers. However, considerable additional fiscal stress is likely to emerge under a PAYG system as the proportion of the retired elderly rises. And if, as is typically the case, the PAYG scheme also involves various redistributive elements, there is further potential for fiscal stress, especially as the population ages. A failure to address the resulting fiscal stresses, coming on top of an already burdensome fiscal situation, could inflict serious macroeconomic and structural damage, both on the domestic economy and, in the case of large industrial countries through international linkages, on the world economy.

The potentially serious fiscal, economic, and social consequences of population aging raise complex issues, not least of which are political issues that arise whenever the distributional impact of a major public program is reconsidered. In principle, individuals should be responsible for making adequate provision for their own retirement. In practice, this has not been judged appropriate for a variety of reasons, necessitating publicly supported schemes. In fact, public pension schemes are widely credited with having led to significant reductions of poverty rates among the elderly. Nevertheless, the issue of how the burden of supporting the aged is to be distributed may become particularly contentious as the proportion of the working population declines, while at the same time the political strength of the elderly increases.

Four ways have been suggested to ameliorate fiscal stresses from the public pension arrangements: (1) through parametric adjustments of the structural characteristics of the pension system, such as the contribution rate, retirement ages, or pension benefit indexation formulas, possibly combined with building up financial reserves; (2) through systemic reforms, principally by developing a significant, defined-contribution, fully funded pillar inside or outside the existing public pension scheme; (3) by undertaking broader fiscal adjustments such as raising taxes and cutting expenditures not related to public pensions; and (4) by modifying the macroeconomic profile by changing such aspects as the size of the labor force through, for example, encouraging greater labor force participation, or immigration. While this study emphasizes approaches (1) and (2), it also considers aspects of approaches (3) and (4).

Growing recognition of the potential consequences of population aging has prompted widespread discussion of the problems and of what to do about them (see Appendix II). Among the most recent studies, a World Bank (1994) report forcefully advocates moving to a three-pillar system for providing old age security: a mandatory publicly managed pillar with the limited goal of reducing poverty among the elderly; a mandatory privately managed pillar providing fully funded pensions; and a voluntary savings pillar. In many industrial countries, adopting the proposed multi-pillar approach would amount to the effective dissolution of present public pension arrangements. Focusing on the need for pension reform in the major industrial countries, OECD studies by Van den Noord and Herd (1993 and 1994) and Leibfritz and others (1995) report estimates of unfunded public pension liabilities under present pension arrangements and discuss the effectiveness of selected parametric reforms. The OECD studies find that raising retirement ages would make a particularly significant contribution to reducing projected unfunded pension liabilities in the major industrial countries. Finally, Masson and Mussa (1995) review the implications of population aging for fiscal policy and conclude that restoring fiscal policy to a sustainable path would necessitate sizable cuts in the extensive commitments for social spending in many industrial countries.

This study examines the pension-related aging problem primarily from a fiscal perspective. The key questions asked are the following. How will prospective demographic developments that affect the proportion of the pensionable elderly affect pension outlays? What is the likely size of the fiscal burdens? What are the fiscal implications of alternative reform approaches for ameliorating the effects of aging on public pensions? The present study, employing a more disaggregated methodology than typically found in other studies, confirms that very serious fiscal stresses are in prospect for most industrial economies. Addressing such problems satisfactorily will require major actions early, given the long lead times involved in reforming a pension fund's financial position. In comparison with the mentioned OECD studies, the present paper seeks to provide a more detailed quantitative assessment of unfunded public pension liabilities and the fiscal implications of parametric reforms. As regards systemic reform proposals aimed at adoption of a fully funded system, this study attempts to evaluate quantitatively the fiscal implications of such reforms in the major industrial countries and in Sweden.[1]

The assessments show that a combination of parametric reductions in benefits, such as extending the retirement age and modifying indexation arrangements, would in most countries suffice to contain potentially adverse fiscal developments. An important implication is that if such reforms are combined with the implementation of a sustainable contribution rate (which the benefit-reducing reforms would

bring closer to the actual contribution rate), the reformed public pension systems would be able to cope with the aging problem. In effect, such a system anticipates the demands associated with aging by making funding provisions in advance, thereby reproducing an essential aspect of the fully funded approach, but without requiring the close person-based relationship between individual contributions and benefits that characterizes a fully funded scheme. By levying a constant projected contribution rate through time—the sustainable contribution rate—this system preserves the compact between the generations that is at the core of a PAYG system, as it distributes equally the burden of meeting pensions across the generations. Advance funding has the further advantage of strengthening fiscal discipline if the publication of regular reports on the actuarial status of the pension system heightens awareness of the future cost implications of today's pension benefit promises.

The study also examines the alternative of a fully funded scheme and finds that the fiscal costs of undertaking such a shift may be very high. Meeting these costs may require, in many cases, an amount of fiscal adjustment substantially higher than what would be needed to fix the PAYG system. Hence, unless there are compensating gains, such as a stimulus to overall saving and superior equity implications, it may be preferable to fix the PAYG system instead of shifting to a fully funded system.

Although the focus of this study is primarily on the industrial countries, the examination of key fiscal issues pertains to other countries as well, for some of whom, especially the transition economies, the fiscal stresses have already become acute. It should also be noted that this study does not address the implications of aging for costs not related to pensions, such as on health care or education, which are also likely to be significant.

Before examining the fiscal consequences of public pension schemes, it is useful to review in more detail demographic trends, the nature of social security systems as they relate to pensions, and some of the conclusions reached in the ongoing debate on pension reform. This review is undertaken next in Section II. The approach in this study to identifying fiscal consequences of aging is set out in Section III, together with the results from its application. Section IV examines in detail the reform options noted above for reducing fiscal stress and discusses criteria that bear on the issue of which reform package to choose. Conclusions are presented in Section V. Appendix I describes the methodological framework and the data sources of the study, and Appendix II contains some bibliographical notes.

---

[1]The choice of Sweden as the representative of the smaller industrial countries was in part influenced by its traditional role as a pacesetter in promoting social welfare reforms and its earlier experiencing of the aging problem.

II   Background

Demographic Trends

Projections of demographic trends reflect assumptions about future variations in fertility, life expectancy, and immigration flows.[2] Present rates of fertility (the number of children born to an average woman during her lifetime) differ considerably across the selected industrial countries, ranging from historically low values of 1.3 (Germany, Italy) to highs of 2.1 (United States, Sweden). Over the next four decades, the demographic scenarios assume, perhaps optimistically, that the fertility rate in all countries will converge to the level needed to maintain a stable population, that is, about 2.1. However, trends in fertility rates are notoriously difficult to predict.[3] Although deviations from the fertility assumptions underlying the projections will not affect the projected number of elderly persons, they could nevertheless have sizable effects on the projected number of persons of young and working age. Life expectancy at birth of both sexes is projected to increase by some five years until 2050, with most of the added longevity occurring before 2020. In light of present political realities, net immigration flows in most of the industrial countries are assumed to taper off quickly from observed levels during the early 1990s, falling to zero in most countries after 2005. Only Canada and the United States are assumed to have positive (but declining) net immigration beyond 2005.

Given the assumptions about fertility, life expectancies, and immigration flows, the age structure of populations in the seven major industrial countries and Sweden is projected to change significantly (Table 1). In particular, elderly dependency ratios—defined as the ratio of the population aged 65 and over to the population aged 15 to 64—are expected to increase sharply, although the pace of aging differs across countries.[4] While elderly dependency ratios in 1995 cluster around 20 percent for most industrial countries, by the year 2030 the ratios are projected to more than double in Japan, Germany, Italy, and Canada. In the United States and France, elderly dependency ratios are projected to almost double by 2030. Population aging in the United Kingdom and Sweden, while it starts in 1995 at a relatively advanced level, is projected to be less pronounced, but elderly dependency ratios will nevertheless reach almost 40 percent by 2030. Beyond 2030, elderly dependency ratios are projected to stabilize in all countries except in Japan and Italy, where further increases of more than 10 percentage points are expected to occur.

Chart 1 plots elderly dependency ratios for the selected industrial countries during 1950–2050, providing a historical perspective on projected aging patterns. While elderly dependency ratios in all countries have been rising steadily since the 1950s, Chart 1 also shows that projected dependency ratios in most countries will increase at a historically unusual pace starting around 2010, reflecting the passage of the postwar baby-boom generation into retirement.

The elderly population itself is projected to age considerably over the projection horizon, as indicated by the projected long-term increases in the very elderly ratio—defined as the ratio of the population aged 75 and over to the population aged 65 and over. However, the occurrence of "double aging" in most countries is erratic rather than continuous and, except in Japan, where life expectancies are particularly high, is not expected to become pro-

---

[2]Data on future demographic trends in the major industrial countries and Sweden are taken from the World Bank's *World Population Projections, 1994–95,* by Bos and others (1994). The World Bank population projections are broadly similar to available official intermediate-range demographic projections in the selected industrial countries.

[3]For example, long-range actuarial estimates of public pension trends in the United States of the Board of Trustees of the OASDI Trust Funds (1995) assume an intermediate-range fertility rate of 1.9 while the low- and high-cost pension projections are based on long-run fertility rates of 2.2 and 1.6, respectively. At the same time, historical experience regarding fertility rates in the United States during 1950–90 ranges from a peak of 3.7 in 1957 to a low of 1.7 in 1976.

[4]World Bank (1994), Chapter 1, reviews future demographic trends in developing countries and transition economies, concluding that elderly dependency ratios are also likely to rise steeply in much of Latin America, Eastern Europe, Central Asia, and China.

Table 1. Demographic Trends
(1995 Population = 100)

Country	1995	2000	2010	2020	2030	2050
United States						
Population	100.0	104.8	113.0	119.8	124.7	127.2
Elderly dependency ratio	19.2	19.0	20.4	27.6	36.8	38.4
Very elderly ratio	42.7	46.3	45.8	40.5	45.8	55.6
Total dependency ratio	52.7	52.0	50.5	57.4	68.0	68.8
Japan						
Population	100.0	101.3	102.2	100.6	97.6	91.6
Elderly dependency ratio	20.3	24.3	33.0	43.0	44.5	54.0
Very elderly ratio	37.8	38.3	44.5	47.2	56.3	58.1
Total dependency ratio	43.9	47.2	56.7	67.8	70.5	84.0
Germany						
Population	100.0	100.0	97.2	94.2	90.6	81.2
Elderly dependency ratio	22.3	23.8	30.3	35.4	49.2	51.9
Very elderly ratio	40.7	42.7	41.8	48.3	44.1	59.7
Total dependency ratio	46.3	46.7	50.0	57.3	75.1	81.3
France						
Population	100.0	102.2	104.9	106.9	107.8	106.1
Elderly dependency ratio	22.1	23.6	24.6	32.3	39.1	43.5
Very elderly ratio	39.2	43.4	49.6	41.9	48.8	56.6
Total dependency ratio	52.2	52.8	51.2	59.6	67.9	73.6
Italy						
Population	100.0	100.1	98.2	95.3	91.9	82.6
Elderly dependency ratio	23.8	26.5	31.2	37.5	48.3	60.0
Very elderly ratio	38.5	42.8	47.9	48.4	48.0	60.9
Total dependency ratio	45.6	47.8	51.5	58.8	72.7	89.6
United Kingdom						
Population	100.0	101.0	102.2	103.5	103.9	102.0
Elderly dependency ratio	24.3	24.4	25.8	31.2	38.7	41.2
Very elderly ratio	42.9	46.3	46.3	44.5	45.8	57.2
Total dependency ratio	54.3	54.0	52.3	58.3	68.0	71.2
Canada						
Population	100.0	105.0	113.2	119.7	123.1	122.7
Elderly dependency ratio	17.5	18.2	20.4	28.4	39.1	41.8
Very elderly ratio	39.9	43.3	44.6	40.2	44.4	55.8
Total dependency ratio	48.6	48.3	47.5	56.3	69.0	71.9
Sweden						
Population	100.0	101.8	103.8	105.7	107.0	107.0
Elderly dependency ratio	27.4	26.9	29.1	35.6	39.4	38.6
Very elderly ratio	46.6	50.8	46.7	45.8	52.2	58.8
Total dependency ratio	56.9	57.9	58.5	65.1	70.4	68.8

Source: Bos and others (1994).

Notes: The *elderly dependency ratio* is defined as population aged 65 and over as a percent of the population aged 15–64. The *very elderly ratio* is defined as the population aged 75 and over as a percent of the population aged 65 and over. The *total dependency ratio* is defined as the population aged 0–14 and 65 and over as a percent of the population aged 15–64.

nounced before 2030. Total dependency ratios—defined as the population aged 0 to 14 and 65 and over to the population aged 15 to 64—are projected to rise significantly less than elderly dependency ratios, indicating that the relative size of the young dependent population is expected to decline over the projection horizon.

Although there is considerable uncertainty about long-term demographic change, the short-term demographic outlook is relatively certain. For example, barring significant migration flows, labor force growth in the next two decades is largely given by past fertility experience and, absent significant unexpected changes in life expectancies, the number of

Chart I. Elderly Dependency Ratios
(In percent)

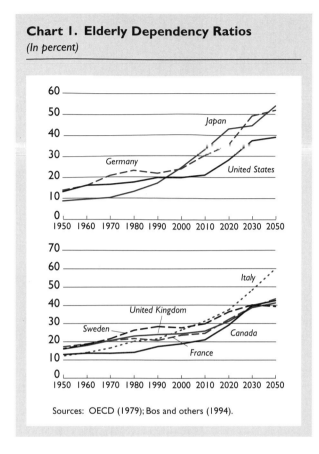

Sources: OECD (1979); Bos and others (1994).

elderly persons can be projected with confidence as far out as the middle of the next century.

Public Pension Arrangements

The main pillar of the old-age security system in most industrial countries is a mandatory public pension plan, which, however, is often complemented by private pension schemes. Mandatory public pension plans are generally based on the defined-benefit principle, according to which the benefit received by the individual is specified in advance, usually as a function of the person's earnings history and the number of contribution years. Pension plans can alternatively be based on the defined-contribution principle, according to which the annual contribution paid by the individual is specified, usually as a proportion of gross salary, and benefits depend on accumulated contributions and the realized rates of return on their past investments.

Public pension expenditures in the major industrial countries and Sweden have increased sharply since 1960, reflecting the rise in the elderly dependency ratios depicted in Chart 1, an increase in the generosity of per capita pensions, and the maturation of public pension schemes.[5] At the same time, estimates of total public pension expenditures at the beginning of the 1990s indicate that public pension expenditures (as a percent of GDP) vary widely across the countries considered in this study, being significantly higher in the selected continental European countries than in the other countries (Table 2). In addition, public pension systems often comprise a wide range of different pension schemes including pension plans for civil servants and particular professions (miners, agricultural workers).[6] Table 2 also provides estimates of the amount of such public pension expenditures covered by the projections of the present study. As the coverage for most countries is significantly less than 100 percent, mainly reflecting data availability, the projections of the study are likely to understate the actual size of net pension liabilities.

Table 3 summarizes selected characteristics of the main public pension schemes in the major industrial countries and Sweden. As regards financing, pension plans can be classified into fully funded, partially funded, or PAYG schemes. In a fully funded scheme, the contribution rate is chosen so as to accumulate a stock of capital that, at any point in time, should equal the present discounted value of future benefits minus future contributions of those currently in the scheme. In a PAYG scheme, benefits accruing to the current beneficiaries are financed by current contributions or budget transfers. A partially funded scheme combines features of a fully funded and a PAYG scheme (but where reserves do not fully meet the aforementioned financial condition). A defined-contribution plan is usually fully funded. Recent pension reform proposals in some countries including Sweden and Latvia seek to mimic the close link between contributions and benefits associated with defined-contribution plans without, however, building up a fund (so-called notional funding). Defined-benefit plans, on the other hand, are most often organized as either PAYG or partially funded. Public pension schemes in many industrial countries, including Germany, France, Italy, the United Kingdom, and Canada, are financed on a PAYG basis, whereas the United States, Japan, and Sweden have adopted

---

[5]OECD (1988a), Table 2.4, provides a breakdown of the influence of the mentioned factors on the change in public expenditure ratios in industrial countries over the period 1960–85.

[6]Kuné and others (1993) provide separate estimates of unfunded pension liabilities of civil servant pension schemes in the European Union countries.

Table 2. Public Pension Expenditure
(In percent of GDP)

| Country | Public Pension Expenditure in 1990[1] | Of Which: | |
		Covered by projections of this study	Not covered by projections of this study
United States	6.9	4.5	2.4
Japan	5.7	5.0	0.7
Germany[2]	12.3	8.9	3.4
France[2]	13.3	11.9	1.4
Italy	14.2	13.9	0.3
United Kingdom	6.4	4.2	2.2
Canada	6.0	3.8	2.2
Sweden	11.3	7.0	4.3

Sources: OECD; and IMF staff estimates.

[1]Defined as spending by all public sector pension schemes including civil service pensions and schemes for specific professions (miners, agricultural workers).

[2]1992.

partially funded schemes.[7] Systems financed exclusively or partially on a PAYG basis are particularly vulnerable to population aging.

The main financing source of public pension schemes is social security contributions levied on gross wage earnings, at statutory rates ranging from 5 percent in Canada to over 27 percent in Italy. In some countries, the contribution is shared equally by the employer and the employee, whereas in others the employer bears more than half of the burden.[8] Most public pension schemes also stipulate that contributions on earnings are only paid up to a specified limit.[9] To the extent that social security contributions fall short of pension expenditure, PAYG systems necessitate transfers from other budgets to cover the shortfall.

Eligibility for pension benefits is typically determined by a statutory retirement age and a minimum contribution period. The United States, Germany, Canada, and Sweden have statutory retirement ages of 65 years for both sexes, while the other countries maintain differentiated statutory retirement ages for men and women. At the same time, most public pension schemes contain provisions for early retirement,

implying that effective retirement ages are often significantly below statutory ones. Some countries, including the United States and Germany, allow for flexible retirement. In particular, an individual can retire before reaching the statutory retirement age, provided that he has reached a minimum pensionable age and paid contributions for a minimum period, and at the cost of a reduction in the benefits proportional to the difference between the individual's age and the statutory retirement age.

In defined-benefit plans, benefits can be earnings related, flat rate, or means tested. Earnings-related benefits are computed on the basis of (1) determination of assessed income: the initial benefit for new retirees is usually computed as a percentage of average wage income assessed over a period that can vary from a few years to the entire career; (2) accrual rate: in most defined-benefit plans, the initial pension is calculated by applying to the assessed income an accrual rate multiplied by the number of years in which the person has contributed to the plan. Accrual rates vary from 0.4 percent in the United Kingdom to 2 percent in Italy. A ceiling is often imposed in the form of a maximum replacement rate, that is, a maximum ratio of the pension benefit to the assessed income. In flat-rate schemes, the benefit is independent of past earnings, but can be tied to other characteristics of beneficiaries. For example, social security arrangements in Japan, the United Kingdom, and Sweden combine earnings-related and flat-rate schemes.

Another important feature of a pension scheme is the type of indexation mechanism for existing pension benefits. In most industrial countries, pension

---

[7]The choice of this widely used terminology is somewhat loose insofar as the funding, for example, in the United States, is intended to smooth out fluctuations in contribution rates rather than create assets that could be assigned to individuals as in a fully funded, defined-contribution scheme.

[8]The United States, Japan, Germany, and Canada are examples of the first category and France, Italy, and Sweden of the second.

[9]All major industrial countries except Italy have maximum earnings ceilings for all or the most significant portions of the pension system.

Table 3. Public Pension Schemes

Country	Financing[1]	Retirement Ages[2] (Men/Women)	Contribution Period for Full Pension	Benefit Accrual Factor[3]	Assessed Earnings	Maximum Replacement Rate	Indexation of Benefits
United States	PF	65/65	35	[4]	Career	41.0	Prices
Japan	PF	60/55	40	0.75	Career	30.0	Net wages
Germany	PAYG	65/65	40	1.50	Career	60.0	Net wages
France[5]	PAYG	60/60	38	1.75	Best 12 years	50.0	Prices/Gross wages
Italy	PAYG	62/57	40	2.00	Last 5 years	80.0	Prices
United Kingdom	PAYG	65/60	50	0.40	Career	20.0	Prices
Canada[6]	PAYG	65/65	40	0.50	Career	25.0	Prices
Sweden[6]	PF	65/65	30	[7]	Best 15 years	60.0	Prices

Sources: Van den Noord and Herd (1993), Table 1.1; and IMF staff estimates.

[1]PAYG = Pay-As-You-Go. PF = Partially Funded.

[2]Statutory retirement ages as of 1995.

[3]Benefit accrual factor per year of contributions, in percent of assessed earnings.

[4]Benefit accrual factor increases as assessed earnings decline.

[5]The basic scheme is indexed to prices, while the earnings-related schemes are indexed to gross wages.

[6]For earnings-related scheme only.

[7]Benefit accrual factor declines as number of contribution years increases.

benefits are indexed to the inflation rate, as measured by the consumer price index (CPI). Among the selected industrial countries, only Japan and Germany use indexation schemes that link existing pensions to the growth rate of net wages, which in the case of Germany is defined as net of payroll and income taxes. In France, the earnings-related pension scheme is indexed to gross wages.

In many industrial countries, private pension schemes complement mandatory public pension plans. However, estimates of the size of accumulated assets of private pension funds at the of end of 1991 differed significantly across the selected industrial countries, ranging from over 70 percent of GDP in the United Kingdom to less than 5 percent of GDP in Germany and France (Table 4). While these estimates are subject to measurement problems, reflecting primarily issues of how to treat life insurance savings and book reserve provisions on companies' balance sheets, available data on asset size nevertheless indicate that countries with relatively low public pension replacement ratios—for example, as measured by the maximum replacement ratios listed in Table 3—have developed sizable private pension schemes.

Pension Reform Debates

At least since the early 1980s, the anticipation of adverse demographic trends has increasingly shaped pension reform debates in industrial coun-

tries.[10] In this context, it is useful to distinguish between two stylized approaches to pension reforms: the "parametric reform approach" and the "systemic reform approach," with some scope for mixing the two.

Parametric Reform Approach

The most widespread reform approach to the aging problem consists in identifying corrective measures that change the parameters of the existing public pension system. A first option is to act on the revenue side. In the past, significant increases in contribution rates have been part of the reforms in many industrial countries, including the United States, Japan, Germany, and Italy. However, as the contribution rates required to restore financial balance have already reached very high levels in some countries, expenditure-reducing measures have increasingly been considered.

Many countries, such as the United States, Japan, Germany, and Italy, have legislated increases in the statutory retirement age to be phased in over a number of years so as to slow down the growth in the number of beneficiaries. In some countries, such as Italy, this has been supplemented by tightening eligibility criteria for early retirement and disability pen-

[10]A comprehensive up-to-date bibliography on pension issues is provided by World Bank (1994). A list of selected references focusing primarily on the public pension systems and reform debates in industrial countries is contained in Appendix II.

Table 4. Assets and Workforce Coverage of Private Pension Funds

Country	Assets (In percent of GDP)[1]		Workforce Coverage (In percent)
	Narrowly defined[2]	Broadly defined[3]	
United States	51.0	66.0	46.0
Japan[4]	5.0	8.0	50.0
Germany[4]	3.0	4.0	42.0
France	2.0	5.0	...
Italy	6.0	...	5.0
United Kingdom	60.0	73.0	50.0
Canada	32.0	35.0	41.0

Source: Davis (1993), Tables 3.1 and 3.4.
[1] At the end of 1991.
[2] Funded pension schemes.
[3] Funded pension schemes and pension resources of life insurers.
[4] In Japan and Germany, large funded pension plans are held directly on firms' balance sheet.

sions. Other expenditure-reducing measures aim at lowering the level of per capita benefits by modifying either the mechanism determining the initial benefit for new pensioners, or the indexation of benefits of existing pensioners. The initial pension benefit in an earnings-related system can be modified in several ways: (1) extending the period of a worker's earning history used for establishing the assessed income for determining the initial pension; (2) adopting partial rather than full grossing up of past earnings in computing the assessed income for determining initial pension levels; (3) reducing the accrual rate; and (4) imposing, or lowering, a maximum replacement rate. The subsequent evolution of the initial pension benefit is affected by whether pension benefits are indexed to prices or to wages (net or gross). The debate on the choice between price and wage indexation is usually centered on the issue of whether or not pensioners should also enjoy the benefits of growth in labor productivity taking place after they have left the labor force. Indexation to net wages ensures that the growth of pension benefits takes account of the impact of higher contribution rates. In order to limit pension expenditures, in 1992, Italy adopted indexation to prices, in place of gross wages, whereas Germany in 1992 and Japan in 1994 shifted to indexation of net rather than gross wage growth.

Systemic Reform Approach

A second approach to the aging problem has involved an increase in the extent to which a PAYG, defined-benefit system is established as a partially or fully funded system; more systemic reforms have in-

volved either the adoption of a more significant defined-contribution element in the pension system, or a full-scale replacement of the defined-benefit approach with a defined-contribution system.[11]

Proposals in favor of a shift to a partially or a fully funded public pension system generally arise from the beliefs that it is the financing mechanism of a PAYG system that lies at the root of the imbalance, and that the development of financial reserves (through partial or full funding) would reduce the need for unsustainable increases in payroll tax or contribution rates. The validity of this approach is not without controversy. If the financial reserves of a public pension system are heavily invested in government securities and there is some bunching in the rate of investment of these securities to pay for annuities, some fiscal strains may be generated, as future taxpayers may have to bear higher tax rates to service the government's debt. In addition, the provision of government-guaranteed minimum rates of return could give rise to contingent government liabilities.

Another argument sometimes made in favor of partially or fully funded schemes is that reserves accumulated under these schemes could constitute a net addition to overall savings in the economy. The empirical issue of the extent to which public pension schemes affect the national savings rate is, however, controversial, as is the issue of the optimal appropri-

---

[11] Most industrial, Latin American and transition countries currently adopt the defined-benefit option, sometimes within a partially funded system. Defined-contribution schemes have been adopted in several Latin American (notably Chile), Asian, and African countries. See World Bank (1994), Table A.7.

ate use of such funds in the general economic context. These issues are discussed in greater detail in Section IV.

A more fundamental systemic reform of the public pension system consists in reallocating responsibilities to the private sector and individuals. "Privatization of social security" is often proposed as a way to mitigate labor market distortions owing to a potentially loose link between benefits and contributions under public pension schemes, to take advantage of the conceivably better rate-of-return characteristics of privatized fully funded schemes, to increase savings and the capital stock of the economy, and to reduce the risk of political mismanagement.[12] Whether the wholesale transition from a PAYG system to a privatized fully funded defined-contribution system would indeed result in sizable net welfare gains for existing or future generations has been examined in several recent theoretical contributions and simulation studies.[13] Using a stylized dynamic life-cycle model, the study by Kotlikoff (1995) in particular has concluded that the size and even sign of net welfare gains from the transition to a privatized pension system depend sensitively on the existing contribution structure, the link between benefits and contributions under the existing system, and the financing of the transition cost.

[12]See Feldstein (1996).

[13]See, for example, Homburg (1990) and Kotlikoff (1995).

The role of private provision of retirement income may also be enhanced by reforms that do not necessarily aim at a wholesale transition to a private fully funded system. In the United Kingdom, for example, members of occupational pension schemes may contract out of the state earnings-related additional pension scheme, thereby reducing the importance of the public pension component. Individual retirement accounts, already a familiar feature of the U.S. and Canadian systems, have recently been introduced in France. And recent social security reform proposals in the United States advocate putting a portion of the contributions of insured workers into mandatory individual or personal retirement accounts to take advantage of higher rates of returns in equity markets.[14]

In those cases where the reform has involved a major structural shift from a defined benefit to a defined contribution approach (such as in Chile), many important transition issues arise, including the treatment of the pension rights already accrued to existing pensioners and current members of the labor force. The solution that is most often proposed is to convert the accrued rights into a bond (so-called recognition bonds) to be issued to qualifying beneficiaries. These rights may, however, be quite sizable, as is indicated subsequently by the results of this study, so that their conversion into financial instruments would raise a number of rather complex issues.

[14]See Gramlich (1996).

III   Identifying Fiscal Consequences

This section outlines the analytical and empirical approach adopted for assessing the long-run fiscal impact of a public pension system.[15] The section also presents projections of the fiscal consequences of preserving current public pension arrangements.

The Approach

As virtually all of the major industrial countries operate some version of a public defined-benefit pension system (mostly on a PAYG basis), either in isolation or in combination with other pension arrangements, an approach to assessing the fiscal implications of such systems requires a modeling of the basic features of the public pension scheme for each country and then undertaking simulations.

In a public pension, defined-benefit system, pensions to the retired elderly are almost wholly financed from the contributions paid by the working population, usually expressed as a proportion of total wages, as well as from budgetary transfers. By definition, in a full-fledged PAYG system, the two determinants of the equilibrium average contribution rate needed to provide for pension payments are (1) the support ratio, defined as the number of contributing workers per pensioner, and (2) the average replacement rate, defined as the proportion of the average wage that is replaced by the average pension.[16] Obviously, the fewer workers there are relative to the number of retired persons, the higher is the average contribution rate needed to cover the overall cost of pension outlays. Similarly, the more generous are pension benefits, as measured by a higher replacement rate, the higher contribution rates will have to be.

Demographic factors and employment conditions, together with the prescribed retirement ages, determine the overall size of the support ratio. To illustrate the effect of demographic factors, consider first a population with an unchanging age structure. For this benchmark case, the flow of payments from the working population would, at an appropriate predefined contribution rate, be just sufficient to cover payments. Continuing with the illustration, assuming that three fifths of the population fall in the working-age group, one fifth are children, and the remaining one fifth are retirees, the stable support ratio would be three workers to one retiree. If the replacement ratio is set at one half of the average wage, a contribution rate of one sixth of the wage—the equilibrium contribution rate—would suffice to cover benefit payments.[17] Assuming that the share of labor amounted to two thirds of GDP, the flow of contributions as a percentage of GDP would then amount to just over 11 percent, which is the amount needed to cover the consumption needs of the pensioners at the assumed replacement level.

Next suppose an aging population, with the share of the elderly increasing. This will decrease the support ratio, and, if the replacement rate is kept unchanged, necessitate an increase in the contribution rate in order to finance pension outlays. However, the approach adopted in this paper also allows for changes in the replacement rate as a consequence of aging itself, adjustments in the benefit or contribution formulas, including the age of retirement, and movements in average earnings. With regard to aging, the methodology developed is fairly comprehensive, in that it attempts to take a fuller account of demographic developments, tracing effects through different age cohorts of the earnings history and other characteristics that may be unique to a particular age group. The average replacement rate over the

---

[15]The model underlying the projections is detailed in Appendix I.

[16]Formally, the average pension and average social security contribution are assumed to be fixed proportions α (average contribution rate) and β (average replacement rate) of the same average earnings base (W). Assuming there are M pensioners and N workers, revenue and expenditure of the PAYG system are given by $N\alpha W$ and $M\beta W$, respectively. Accordingly, setting $N\alpha W = M\beta W$, the equilibrium contribution rate of a PAYG system is defined as $\alpha = \beta(M/N)$, where (M/N) is the system dependency ratio. The inverse of (M/N) is called the support ratio (S), and the equilibrium contribution rate can therefore be calculated equivalently as $\alpha = (\beta/S)$.

[17]As indicated before, the equilibrium contribution rate is determined as the product of the system dependency ratio and the replacement ratio, which in the present example yields $\frac{1}{6} = \frac{1}{3} \times \frac{1}{2}$.

Table 5. Projections of Averages of Macroeconomic Variables, 1995–2050
(In percent)

	Employment Growth	Real GDP Growth	Real Interest Rate	Inflation Rate
Major industrial countries	−0.1	1.4	3.5	3.0
United States	0.3	1.7	3.5	3.0
Japan	−0.6	1.1	3.5	3.0
Germany	−0.8	1.1	3.5	3.0
France	−0.2	1.3	3.5	3.0
Italy	−0.6	0.8	3.5	3.0
United Kingdom	−0.1	1.4	3.5	3.0
Canada	0.1	1.6	3.5	3.0
Sweden	—	1.3	3.5	3.0

Source: IMF staff estimates.

projection period will thus vary, reflecting the changing income characteristics of the cohorts.

A full general-equilibrium approach is, however, not adopted. In particular, the projection model does not endogenize the labor force's reaction, or the savings response of the private sector, to changes in public pension arrangements. Such responses could be significant; for example, an increase in contribution rates could be sufficiently distortive so as to lower the supply of labor, thereby increasing the system dependency ratio; in a similar vein, increased pension expenditure could crowd out private capital accumulation and make it more difficult for the economy to support a larger aged population.

A further important assumption that may affect the results of the study is the choice of the projection horizon. The present study uses 2050 as the cutoff year for the projections, roughly comparable to projection horizons used in other studies.[18] The selected projection horizon reflects a somewhat arbitrary compromise between the objective of capturing the full fiscal ramifications of the transition to a new "population steady state" and the increasing margin of uncertainty that attaches to projections that reach farther and farther into the future. The most likely effect of extending the projection horizon beyond 2050 would be to enlarge the estimated net pension liabilities, as all countries except the United Kingdom are projected to have primary pension fund deficits in 2050.

To make the analysis more tractable, certain plausible assumptions are imposed regarding the rate of growth of the labor force (and the implied participation and employment rates) taking into account preannounced increases in retirement ages, the rate of capital accumulation and the implied rate of private saving, and the rate of total factor productivity growth, and hence the underlying nature and rates of technological progress. This approach has the advantage of not relegating the determination of key macroeconomic variables, whose interaction with pension arrangements is, to say the least, controversial, to a "general equilibrium black box." Moreover, the assumptions made can be easily replaced by others, which can then be used to assess the sensitivity of the results, as is done subsequently.

Table 5 lists the main macroeconomic projections. Among the features of note in the table are: (1) for most countries, employment growth is projected to be negative as a consequence of aging, and even for the United States and Canada, employment growth, which is boosted by immigration, is projected to be low; (2) these employment projections constrain real GDP growth to be low, despite assuming a relatively high rate of multi-factor productivity growth and some capital deepening;[19] and (3) the real interest rate is projected to be substantially higher than the projected real GDP growth rate, indicating that the projected long-run growth path is dynamically efficient,[20] but also that fiscal accounts will have to ex-

---

[18]Recent public pension spending projections for Germany and France (*PROGNOS-Gutachten* (1995) and *Livre Blanc* (1991), respectively) use 2040 as the endyear. The projection horizons of the Government Actuary's (1990) study for the United Kingdom and the Board of Trustees' (1995) study for the United States employed 2050 and 2070 as final years, respectively. A recent OECD study by Leibfritz and others (1995) used 2070 as the cutoff year.

[19]Real GDP growth reflects a Cobb-Douglas production function with exogenous labor-augmenting technical progress, the latter growing at 1.5 percent per year in all countries (see Appendix I).

[20]A long-run growth path is said to be "dynamically efficient" if the real interest rate is equal to or greater than the real growth rate. In a dynamically inefficient economy, the capital stock is "too large" in the sense that society could increase present consumption without lowering the welfare of future generations.

Table 6. Projections of Pension Replacement Rates, Support Ratios, and Contribution Rates

	1995	2000	2010	2030	2050
Major industrial countries					
Replacement rate	37.5	37.1	35.4	35.8	35.1
Support ratio	3.2	3.2	3.0	2.0	1.8
Equilibrium rate	13.7	14.1	13.8	21.5	22.6
Projected rate	13.4	13.4	13.4	13.4	13.4
United States					
Replacement rate	38.5	37.7	35.1	36.8	36.6
Support ratio	4.2	4.3	4.1	2.5	2.3
Equilibrium rate	9.1	8.8	8.6	15.0	15.9
Projected rate	9.7	9.7	9.7	9.7	9.7
Japan					
Replacement rate	19.6	19.8	19.2	19.5	19.3
Support ratio	2.6	2.3	2.1	1.8	1.5
Equilibrium rate	7.7	8.7	9.3	10.8	12.7
Projected rate	5.6	5.6	5.6	5.6	5.6
Germany					
Replacement rate	52.0	51.0	49.0	48.8	48.7
Support ratio	2.3	2.1	2.0	1.2	1.2
Equilibrium rate	22.6	25.0	24.7	41.1	41.6
Projected rate	22.8	22.8	22.9	22.9	22.9
France					
Replacement rate	60.1	59.4	59.5	59.8	59.5
Support ratio	2.5	2.6	2.4	1.6	1.4
Equilibrium rate	24.3	23.2	24.4	37.7	41.2
Projected rate	23.4	23.4	23.4	23.4	23.4
Italy					
Replacement rate	53.9	55.8	55.6	53.7	50.8
Support ratio	1.3	1.2	1.4	0.9	0.7
Equilibrium rate	42.6	45.5	40.4	61.9	68.2
Projected rate	42.6	42.6	42.6	42.6	42.6
United Kingdom					
Replacement rate	17.5	17.4	16.8	14.4	10.6
Support ratio	2.7	2.7	2.5	2.1	2.1
Equilibrium rate	6.4	6.4	6.8	6.9	5.0
Projected rate	6.2	6.2	6.2	6.2	6.2
Canada					
Replacement rate	29.2	28.4	25.6	22.6	20.1
Support ratio	3.6	3.5	2.9	1.7	1.6
Equilibrium rate	8.1	8.2	8.9	13.7	12.9
Projected rate	5.7	5.7	5.7	5.9	6.0
Sweden					
Replacement rate	39.0	38.3	34.3	29.0	23.8
Support ratio	2.6	2.7	2.5	1.8	1.9
Equilibrium rate	14.8	14.1	14.0	15.9	12.8
Projected rate	12.3	12.3	12.3	12.3	12.3

Source: IMF staff estimates.

Notes: The *replacement rate* is defined as the average pension benefit as a percent of average gross wage. The *support ratio* is defined as the ratio of contributors to beneficiaries. The *equilibrium rate* is the contribution rate including net budget transfers (as a percent of wage bill) that maintains year-by-year financial balance of the pension system. The *projected rate* is the projected contribution rate including net budgetary transfers (as a percent of wage bill).

hibit sizable primary surpluses for public debt ratios to be sustainable.

The implications of a PAYG scheme can be assessed by first examining how required contribution rates will need to evolve over the projected period to provide for benefits. This is shown by movements of the "equilibrium rate" in Table 6, or the proportion of the average wage that has to be contributed to just cover pension benefits as determined by replacement rates and support ratios. The table shows substantial increases in the equilibrium contribution rate for all countries except the United Kingdom and Sweden. For the latter countries, the declining equilibrium contribution rates reflect the assumed indexation of all flat-rate pension benefits (for new and pre-existing pensioners) to CPI inflation and a less pronounced deterioration in the support ratios.[21] While Canada also indexes flat-rate benefits to CPI inflation, the decline in the support ratio more than offsets the projected fall in the replacement rate, which causes the equilibrium contribution rate to continue rising.

To assume that equilibrating adjustments will always take the form of further increases in contribution rates is problematic, as considerable resistance is likely to be encountered from contributing generations to further hikes in contribution rates, especially when these are already high. Keeping contribution rates and associated budgetary support constant at current levels could, however, lead to highly adverse future fiscal circumstances. To bring this aspect out fully in a manner that also sheds light on the possible need for pension reform, the approach pursued here is to keep contribution rates and any net budget transfers at their present levels—the "projected rate" in Table 6—and to then examine the potential fiscal consequences. This is undertaken by estimating the implied accumulation of unfunded liabilities.

The approach proceeds by first constructing a baseline using the "projected-contribution rate," and then asks what the fiscal implications for the public pension fund are. Depending on the time horizon of the analysis and the demographics, the result could be a persistent deficit that results in a growing net liability position. Through simulations, the analytical framework can then be used to answer questions involving parametric reforms, such as by how much the contribution rate would have to rise to eliminate the increased net liability position, or what the potential impact would be of alternative policy choices, such as adjusting benefits and extending the retirement ages.

Evaluating the fiscal consequences of a change to a fully funded system raises a number of issues. To

determine the fiscal costs, the study seeks to identify initially the size of the unfunded liabilities associated with existing and prospective pensioners in the current systems. The sizes involved will of course depend on the arrangements that are made as to how the transition from a defined-benefit, PAYG system takes place. The two polar alternative scenarios considered here are (1) the "sudden" transition, where the switch to a fully funded, defined-contribution system is made at one point in time and applies to all current pensioners, who are "cashed out," and future beneficiaries; and (2) the "gradual" transition, where only new entrants to the labor force after the selected date of conversion become members of a fully funded, defined-contribution scheme.

In the latter case, the transition may take many years depending on the survival rates for beneficiaries still subject to the defined-benefit, PAYG system. Regardless of which approach is adopted, and the variants in between, the effect of taking the decision to move to a fully funded, defined-contribution system is to make explicit the unfunded liabilities of the PAYG system. Recognizing the full extent of these liabilities as a stock at one point in time raises more immediately the issue of how this debt is to be dealt with.

Projected Fiscal Positions Under Present Arrangements

The methodology described above is employed to assess how aging affects public pension expenditures under present arrangements that include known future changes in the structure of benefits. Table 7 and Chart 2 show projected levels of pension expenditures as a percentage of GDP. The table and Chart 3 present the balance in each of these years between the flows of expenditures and revenues (including interest on net assets) from contributions, including any budgetary support provided at the levels established at the start of the projection period as a fixed percentage of GDP. As shown in Table 7 and Chart 4, these annual flows will have implications for the net asset position of the (implicit) reserve funds associated with the pension arrangements. For the United States, Japan, and Sweden, these are explicit reserve funds; for the other countries, these reserves are implicitly attributed by the assumed methodology.

The qualitative thrust of the results confirms the findings of previous studies such as Leibfritz and others (1995). All the listed countries, with the exception of the United Kingdom and Sweden, exhibit rising shares of public pension expenditures in GDP. Maintaining contribution rates at the projected levels results, again with the exception of these two countries, in a considerable worsening of public pension

---

[21]Indexation of flat-rate pension benefits for new and pre-existing pensioners to CPI inflation implies a secular fall in replacement rates, raising the issue of political sustainability of this particular indexation arrangement. However, if flat-rate pension benefits of new pensioners are indexed to wages, the financial outlook is considerably less favorable. For example, in the case of the United Kingdom, the projected equilibrium contribution rate under the alternative indexation arrangement rises to 10 percent by 2040 (compared with the 6.9 percent rate shown in Table 6) before declining to 8.8 percent in 2050 (compared with 5.0 percent in Table 6).

Table 7. Baseline Projections of Pension Expenditure, Balances, and Net Asset Positions of Public Pension Funds

(In percent of GDP)

Country	1995	2000	2010	2030	2050
Major industrial countries					
Pension expenditure	6.7	6.9	7.0	10.7	11.4
Balance	0.5	0.2	−0.3	−6.6	−15.5
Net assets	8.3	5.6	−1.1	−61.6	−209.7
United States					
Pension expenditure	4.4	4.3	4.2	7.4	7.7
Balance	0.8	1.1	1.7	−2.2	−7.2
Net assets	7.0	9.5	17.2	3.0	−66.7
Japan					
Pension expenditure	5.7	6.5	7.5	8.9	10.7
Balance	1.1	−0.4	−4.1	−10.9	−23.4
Net assets	26.5	13.9	−17.1	−144	−399.2
Germany					
Pension expenditure	10.0	11.1	11.0	18.4	18.7
Balance	0.2	−0.9	−1.3	−14.9	−34.7
Net assets	1.1	−0.1	−8.8	−115.6	−431.3
France					
Pension expenditure	12.5	12.0	12.6	19.4	21.3
Balance	−0.5	—	−0.4	−13.2	−31.5
Net assets	−0.5	−1.2	0.6	−100.5	−369.6
Italy					
Pension expenditure	16.0	17.1	15.2	23.3	25.7
Balance	—	−1.1	−1.1	−8.8	−18.4
Net assets	—	−16.9	−29.9	−186.8	−338.2
United Kingdom					
Pension expenditure	4.4	4.3	4.6	4.7	3.4
Balance	−0.2	−0.2	−0.7	−1.1	−0.2
Net assets	−0.2	—	−4.3	−10.5	−14.5
Canada					
Pension expenditure	4.4	4.5	4.9	7.5	7.1
Balance	−0.2	−0.5	−1.4	−7.6	−14.7
Net assets	7.0	4.0	−5.1	−67.3	−188.8
Sweden					
Pension expenditure	8.5	8.2	8.1	9.2	7.4
Balance	1.3	0.4	0.2	−3.0	−3.8
Net assets	25.8	21.9	18.3	−16.3	−56.7

Source: IMF staff estimates.

fund balances, with the deficits becoming larger as the projection period is lengthened. The problem is especially pronounced for Germany, Japan, France, and Italy, for whom, in addition to the adverse effects of aging, the progressive deterioration in the net asset positions underlying the public pension schemes is a major contributory factor.

Over the projection period, the deteriorating balances overturn a positive net asset position in 1995 for several countries, resulting in a growing stock of accumulated net liabilities. The need to meet the debt-service charges on the accumulated liabilities further aggravates the pension fund balances. While noteworthy for most countries in the sample, it is especially marked for Japan, Germany, France, and Italy, for whom the negative net asset position reaches a multiple of three to four times GDP in 2050. The United Kingdom and Sweden show the least deterioration because of relatively moderate decreases of support ratios and—as already indicated—flat-rate pension benefits of new and pre-existing pensioners are indexed only to CPI infla-

Chart 2. Projected Pension Expenditure of Public Pension Funds

(In percent of GDP)

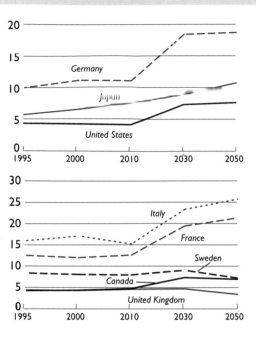

Source: IMF staff estimates.
Note: Projected public pension expenditure under present pension arrangements (see also Table 7) taking account of legislated future increases in statutory retirement ages and based on projections of macroeconomic variables reported in Table 5.

Chart 3. Projected Balances of Public Pension Funds

(In percent of GDP)

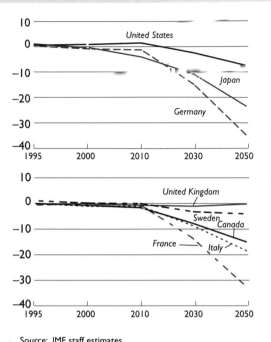

Source: IMF staff estimates.
Note: Balance of public pension fund is defined as difference between projected pension expenditure (Chart 2) and projected revenues from contributions, budgetary transfers, which are kept constant as a percent of GDP at 1995 level, and interest on net pension fund assets.

tion, while contributions are indexed to the rate of nominal wage growth. This latter approach represents a potent combination for preserving the financial integrity of a pension scheme, although at the expense of a major deterioration in the relative income position of pensioners.[22]

Under the assumed conditions, with the exception of the United States, France, and Sweden, all the listed countries would have a negative net asset position by 2010. Subsequently, the United States, France, and Sweden also begin to show negative net asset positions. In the year 2050, even though there is some reversal in elderly dependency ratios, the earlier buildup in the negative net asset positions becomes a dominant factor that, as noted earlier, con-

tributes to a worsening of pension fund balances and thus a further deterioration in the net asset positions.

Sustainable Fiscal Stance and Projected Liabilities

The projected deterioration in pension fund balances under present arrangements and the associated increase in net liabilities aggravates the fiscal position of most major industrial countries. Table 8 shows the net public debt position of the major industrial countries and Sweden at the end of 1994, which ranges from about 33 percent of GDP for Japan to almost 113 percent of GDP for Italy. If account is taken of unfunded pension liabilities, the implied public debt position deteriorates for most of the countries considered. This is evident from column 2 of Table 8, which converts the net asset positions of the previous table to 1995 present values using the interest rates shown in Table 5. The esti-

---

[22]Some illustrations of the effect of CPI indexation on replacement rates are provided in Section IV, Table 14. For example, the replacement rate of a pension with a retirement span of 15 years will decrease by 20 percentage points if labor productivity grows by 1.5 percent.

Chart 4. Projected Net Asset Positions of Public Pension Funds
(In percent of GDP)

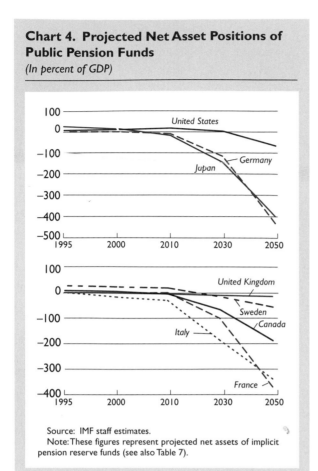

Source: IMF staff estimates.
Note: These figures represent projected net assets of implicit pension reserve funds (see also Table 7).

mated net pension liabilities range from a low of nearly 5 percent of GDP for the United Kingdom to about 110 percent of GDP for Japan, Germany, and France. When added to the end-1994 net public debt positions, the resulting combined net debt position is much worse, exceeding 100 percent of GDP for all countries except the United Kingdom and Sweden.

If one judges the sustainability of a nation's fiscal stance in terms of the conventional criterion of stabilizing net public debt at its current levels, it would appear that the present fiscal stances of Italy and Germany are sustainable: their projected primary balances in 1995 exceed the amounts needed to stabilize the ratio of net public debt (excluding pension liabilities) to GDP. Because assumed real interest rates are higher than projected real growth rates, primary fiscal balances would have to be positive to offset the growth in debt ratios induced by the interest rate. Those other countries for which the primary balances are negative will therefore have to engage in substantial fiscal consolidation just to stabilize their public debt ratios. This is seen by comparing the estimated sustainable primary balances shown in column 5 of Table 8 with their current levels. Sweden, for exam-

ple, would have to improve its primary balance by an estimated 5.2 percent of GDP, while Canada would need to improve it by 2.5 percent of GDP.

However, if account is taken of the projected buildup in net pension debt, and the sustainability criterion is modified to include as well the prevention of any buildup of pension debts, primary balances would have to be even more positive, as is shown by the estimates in column 6. The full amount of the fiscal consolidation needed to both stabilize current net public debt positions and prevent any buildup of pension debts is indicated in the last column of the table. This shows that fiscal consolidation needs become much more stringent for most of the countries. For Germany and Italy, indications under the conventional criterion that their primary balances are adequate are reversed: improvements in primary balances of 2.1 percent of GDP for Germany and 1.3 percent of GDP for Italy are required. For the major industrial countries as a group, an improvement of 2.2 percent of GDP is needed to ensure fiscal sustainability. As a percent of GDP, the greatest need for fiscal consolidation is estimated to arise for Japan, France, and Canada at about 4 percent to 5 percent of GDP and Sweden at 6 percent of GDP. The United States and the United Kingdom manifest smaller needs, both because their current primary balance is close to the levels required to stabilize existing public debt ratios and because the projected buildup of pension debt under current pension arrangements is more modest.

The sought-after improvements in primary balances can be obtained in several ways through adjustments in different revenue and expenditure components. A convenient way of expressing the adjustments needed to prevent any buildup in pension-related debt is to express them as increases in contribution rates at the outset of the projection period—so-called "sustainable contribution rates."[23] Column 1 of Table 9 presents overall public pension contribution rates (defined as a percent of GDP), including net budget transfers, that are expected to prevail in 1995 for the major industrial countries and Sweden. The second column presents the average projected contribution rates ascribable to the entire projection period 1995–2050. By assumption, the average projected contribution rates do not differ from those shown in the first column, ranging from a low of 3.8 percent of GDP for Canada to a high of

---

[23]The "sustainable" rate should be distinguished from the "equilibrium" rate. In the study, the latter refers to the rate, which could change from year to year, for pension fund flows to be in balance. The sustainable rate, in contrast, refers to that constant contribution rate that would, when introduced, preserve intertemporal balance between flows as assessed by the sustainability criterion of no debt buildup over the initial reference point.

Table 8. Net Pension Liabilities and Sustainability of Fiscal Stance
(In percent of GDP)

| | Net Public Debt at End, 1994[1] (1) | Net Pension Liability, 1995–2050[2] (2) | Combined Net Debt Liability (3) | Primary Balance 1995[3] (4) | Sustainable Primary Balance Required to | | Adjustment Needed in Primary Balance for Fiscal Sustainability[6] (7) |
					Stabilize net public debt in 1995[4] (5)	Stabilize net public debt and prevent buildup of pension debt[5] (6)	
Major industrial countries	57.2	60.0	117.2	0.7	1.0	2.9	2.2
United States	63.3	25.7	89.0	0.4	1.1	1.9	1.5
Japan	33.2	106.8	140.0	−0.2	0.3	3.6	3.8
Germany	52.5	110.7	163.2	2.4	1.1	4.5	2.1
France	42.4	113.6	156.0	−0.3	0.7	4.0	4.3
Italy	112.9	75.5	188.4	3.3	2.1	4.6	1.3
United Kingdom	37.7	4.6	42.3	0.4	0.7	0.8	0.4
Canada	71.6	67.8	139.4	0.2	2.7	4.7	4.5
Sweden	54.5	20.4	74.9	−5.1	0.1	1.0	6.1

Source: IMF staff estimates.

[1]Adjusted for net assets of public pension fund at the end of 1994. Estimate of net public debt for Germany includes unification debt as of the end of 1994.

[2]Net present value of difference between projected primary expenditure and revenue of public pension fund during 1995–2050, adjusted for net asset position of public pension systems at the end of 1994.

[3]May 1995 WEO projections of structural primary balance of general government.

[4]Primary balance required to stabilize net public debt in 1995.

[5]Sustainable primary balance in column (5) plus contribution gap from column (4) of Table 9.

[6]Difference between columns (6) and (4).

Table 9. Sustainable Contribution Rates and Contribution Gaps
(In percent of GDP)

	Projected Contribution Rate in 1995[1] (1)	Projected Average Contribution Rate 1995–2050 (2)	Sustainable Contribution Rate 1995–2050[2] (3)	Contribution Gap[3] (4)
Major industrial countries	6.5	6.5	8.3	1.8
United States	4.7	4.7	5.5	0.8
Japan	3.9	3.9	7.2	3.3
Germany	10.3	10.3	13.7	3.4
France	12.1	12.1	15.4	3.3
Italy	16.0	16.0	18.5	2.5
United Kingdom	4.2	4.2	4.3	0.1
Canada	3.8	3.8	5.8	2.0
Sweden	7.1	7.1	8.0	0.9

Source: IMF staff estimates.

[1]Including net budget transfers.

[2]The sustainable contribution rate is defined as the constant contribution rate over 1995–2050 that equalizes the net asset position in 2050 with the initial net asset position in 1995.

[3]Defined as the difference between sustainable contribution rate and projected contribution rate in 1995.

Chart 5. Projected Public Pension Fund Contribution Rates

(In percent of GDP)

16 percent of GDP for Italy.[24] It is noteworthy that these contribution rates are clearly insufficient for the equilibration of the public pension schemes as is indicated by the sustainable contribution rates shown in column 3.

The sustainable contribution rate is for the most part substantially higher than the projected average rate, especially for Italy, where it is estimated to be 18.5 percent of GDP, Germany (13.7 percent of GDP), Japan (7.2 percent of GDP), and France (15.4 percent of GDP).[25] Subtracting the projected contribution rate for 1995 from the sustainable rate

yields estimates of the "contribution gap" that are shown in the fourth column of the table. There is virtually no gap for the United Kingdom and relatively small gaps for Sweden and the United States, as compared to the other countries listed in the table.

In terms of maintaining fiscal viability, alternative options are a once-and-for-all move to the sustainable contribution rate and year-by-year adjustments of contribution rates to equilibrate the pension fund. The alternative profiles of contribution rates (again as a percent of GDP) over the projection horizon in the selected industrial countries are brought out in Chart 5.[26] The chart shows that year-by-year adjustments of contribution rates, while seemingly more attractive in that initial-year rates would be less than their sustainable levels and would aggravate the burden of high contribution rates in the outer years rais-

[24]Accordingly, in the case of Germany, it is assumed that the automatic feedback mechanism to finance anticipated shortfalls in the pension fund introduced by the 1992 Pension Reform Act, which may lead to automatic increases in pension contribution rates and budget transfers, is not operative during the projection period.

[25]Expressed as a percent of the wage bill, as is normal with payroll taxes, the implied contribution rates would, of course, be considerably larger.

[26]The equilibrium contribution rates are taken from Table 6 but have been reexpressed as a percent of GDP.

Chart 5 *(concluded)*

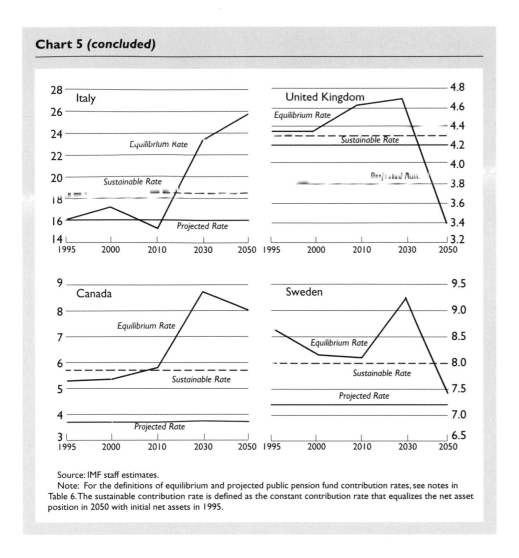

Source: IMF staff estimates.
Note: For the definitions of equilibrium and projected public pension fund contribution rates, see notes in Table 6. The sustainable contribution rate is defined as the constant contribution rate that equalizes the net asset position in 2050 with initial net assets in 1995.

ing issues of efficiency and intertemporal equity. If increases in contribution rates are considered inevitable at some point, the efficiency gains from tax smoothing could, in principle, provide a powerful economic rationale for moving to sustainable contribution rates early on. However, from other quantitative studies, the efficiency gains of tax smoothing associated with earlier moves to sustainable contribution rates are likely to be small.[27] By contrast, intertemporal equity considerations could provide a forceful argument for an early implementation of sustainable contribution rates as it would equally distribute the burden of paying pensions across generations.

---

[27]See, for example, Cutler and others (1990).

Sensitivity Analysis

Using the earlier results as a reference point, it is useful to examine the sensitivity of net pension liabilities and contribution gaps to the real GDP growth rate and the real interest rate. Table 10 presents the results of assuming that the baseline rate of real GDP growth falls by 1.5 percentage points as a result of an equivalent decline in the rate of technical progress; the effect of a reduction in the real rate of interest to 2 percent (from 3.5 percent in the baseline) is also shown.

Interestingly, lower GDP growth has a beneficial effect on net pension liabilities and contribution gaps for those countries for whom pension arrangements involve full or partial indexation of benefits to nominal wages, such as Japan, Germany, and France (the former two to net wages, the latter, for

Table 10. Sensitivity of Estimated Net Pension Liabilities and Contribution Gaps to Real GDP Growth and Interest Rate Assumptions
(In percent of GDP)

	Baseline Projection	Effect on Baseline Projection of	
		Lower real GDP growth[1]	Lower real interest rate[2]
Major industrial countries			
Net pension liability	65.1	−6.9	39.9
Contribution gap	1.8	0.2	0.5
United States			
Net pension liability	25.7	−5.8	24.3
Contribution gap	0.8	−0.1	0.4
Japan			
Net pension liability	106.8	−38.5	43.4
Contribution gap	3.3	−0.8	0.6
Germany			
Net pension liability	110.7	−40.0	78.4
Contribution gap	3.4	−0.7	0.8
France			
Net pension liability	113.6	−22.9	85.6
Contribution gap	3.3	0.2	0.8
Italy			
Net pension liability	75.5	78.6	59.4
Contribution gap	2.5	4.1	0.8
United Kingdom			
Net pension liability	4.6	37.2	0.5
Contribution gap	0.1	1.6	—
Canada			
Net pension liability	67.8	9.3	45.2
Contribution gap	2.0	1.0	0.4
Sweden			
Net pension liability	20.4	20.7	20.8
Contribution gap	0.9	0.9	0.4

Source: IMF staff estimates.
[1]Rate of technical progress set at zero instead of 1.5 percent (baseline assumption), resulting in a reduction of real GDP growth by the same amount.
[2]Real rate of interest set at 2 percent instead of 3.5 percent (baseline assumption).

earnings-related pensions, to gross pensions). For example, in the case of Germany, the estimated net pension liability declines by 40 percentage points. On the other hand, for the pension arrangements of Italy, the United Kingdom, Canada, and Sweden, for whom indexation of benefits is to the CPI, the effects of lower GDP growth are adverse. For the United States, the reduction in GDP growth has only a small (negative) effect on the net pension liability.

Where nominal gross or net wage indexation prevails, lower GDP growth decreases the projected nominal amounts of primary deficits as contributions and expenditure decrease by roughly equipropor-

tionate amounts.[28] As the projected smaller primary deficits are discounted using the same interest rate as in the baseline and are then expressed as a percent of the unchanged level of 1995 GDP, the net pension liability declines in response to lower GDP growth. In contrast, under CPI indexation, pension expenditures may decline significantly less than contributions, resulting in increased projected primary deficits and thus increased net pension liabilities. These sensitiv-

[28]To the extent that pensions of new pensioners reflect an average of past earnings, pension expenditure will fall less than contributions. The simulations indicate that this effect is of minor importance.

Table 11. Effect of Postponement of Pension Reform
(In percent of GDP)

	Baseline	Increase in Contribution Gap If Reforms Are Postponed by			
		5 years	10 years	15 years	30 years
Major industrial countries	1.8	0.3	0.7	1.4	4.5
United States	0.8	0.1	0.2	0.5	1.5
Japan	3.3	0.6	1.4	2.7	8.9
Germany	3.4	0.6	1.3	2.7	9.5
France	3.3	0.6	1.3	2.4	7.9
Italy	2.5	0.5	1.1	1.9	6.5
United Kingdom	0.1	—	0.1	0.1	0.3
Canada	2.0	0.1	0.5	0.9	3.4
Sweden	0.9	0.1	0.2	0.4	1.5

Source: IMF staff estimates.

ity results indicate that depending on the indexation scheme, the level of estimated net pension liabilities (and contribution gaps) may vary inversely with the assumed GDP growth rate, suggesting that these estimates may have to be treated more cautiously as indicators of fiscal stress in public pension systems than is customary in the literature.[29]

The effect of lower real interest rates is found to be uniformly adverse for both net pension liabilities and contribution gaps. The adverse effects are especially severe for Japan, Germany, France, and Italy. The reason is that the projected initial buildup in net assets from imposing sustainable contribution rates, which would subsequently be drawn down to pay for the aging-induced excess of payments over contribution flows, benefits less from interest rate compounding when the rate is lower. While lower real interest rates are desirable for their favorable eco-

nomic effects, they do not directly help resolve pension-related problems. In general, the simulations demonstrate that traditional public pension schemes that index contributions to wages and benefits to CPI inflation are more viable when real GDP growth rates and real interest rates are higher.

Delaying Reforms

In light of the political difficulties associated with pension reform, it is useful to examine the added costs of postponement. Table 11 indicates the increment to the sustainable contribution gaps associated with delay. If reform is postponed by five years, the sustainable contribution gaps would rise but by a relatively modest amount; the largest increment would be for Italy, equaling almost 1 additional percent of GDP. Obviously, the longer the delay, the greater the costs in terms of the amount by which sustainable contribution rates would have to be raised. If, for example, reforms are delayed for 15 years, the contribution gap would in most cases increase by more than two thirds. These results suggest a limited window of opportunity for public pension reforms.

---

[29]By contrast, projected net asset positions of pension funds in the simulation study unambiguously deteriorate under lower GDP growth, independently of the indexation scheme. For example, in the case of Germany, net assets in 2050 under lower GDP growth amount to –581.3 percent of GDP, as compared to –431.3 percent of GDP in the baseline.

IV   Reform Options

The previous section pointed to the need for major pension adjustments for most major industrial countries so as to ensure that their public pension systems are sustainable and to prevent a buildup in pension-related debt. It was further noted in the previous section that improvements in the macroeconomic environment would be helpful. While there may be some scope for fiscal measures not related to pensions, for most countries the emphasis will have to be on reforming the pension arrangements themselves. This section reviews several such reforms, of both a parametric and a systemic nature, and attempts to quantify the fiscal impact of reforms on the financial position of the public pension system. It is more difficult to quantify the effect of reform options on the overall fiscal position. Broadly, most parametric reforms are likely to improve the overall fiscal position of government if there is not much offset from the non-pension part of the budget. By contrast, the overall fiscal balance effect of partial advance funding is more controversial; it has been argued that the accumulation of pension fund reserves may loosen the overall budget constraint, in particular if pension fund surpluses count toward overall deficit reduction. Regarding the overall fiscal impact of systemic reforms, this will partly depend on whether transition costs are financed by debt accumulation or taxes.

Fiscal Reforms Unrelated to Pensions

An examination of the underlying fiscal stances for the major industrial countries and Sweden (Table 8) showed that improvements in primary balances will be needed in several countries to stabilize net public debts. This obviously limits the scope for using general fiscal measures to address the additional burdens imposed by a deteriorating public pension system. Nevertheless, it may at times be advantageous to undertake a reform unrelated to pensions if the choices available with regard to pension reform are not adequate. For example, it may be less distortive to cut government expenditure or even to increase consumption taxes than to raise payroll taxes to contain a pension-related deterioration in fiscal balances. Important issues are raised regarding possible trade-offs between pension and fiscal reforms unrelated to pensions that are, however, beyond the scope of the present paper.

Parametric Reforms

Much of the debate on pension reform has centered on adjustments in existing pension arrangements with respect to different aspects of the contribution and benefit structures. Past parametric pension reforms in many industrial countries routinely resorted to financing pension fund imbalances by increasing revenue, mainly by raising contribution rates but also by increasing budgetary transfers. However, in terms of both equity and efficiency, this course of action has become increasingly controversial. As regards equity, in many industrial countries the substantial increases in social security contribution rates, which in most countries are levied at flat rates up to a specified limit, have worked to undermine the overall progressivity of the tax system.[30] Additionally, raising social security contribution rates to finance social security benefits of the relatively well-off elderly portion of the population has come to be viewed as unfairly burdening low- and moderate-income families. As regards efficiency, increasing already high social security contribution rates has been widely associated with reducing employment, in particular of low-wage labor and of workers with relatively elastic labor supply elasticities.

Confronted by increasing resistance from both wage earners and employers to further hikes in payroll tax rates, the emphasis has shifted increasingly to lowering benefits. However, the latter is resisted by well-organized pensioners, whose numbers are of course rising rapidly. The tendency, therefore, has been to formulate increasingly forward-looking proposals that involve adjusting the benefits of future

---

[30]This assumes that pension contributions are at least partly perceived as a tax and that the economic incidence largely falls on workers.

Table 12. Effect of Changes in Pension Benefit Formulas on Contribution Gaps

(In percent of GDP)

	Baseline Projection	Effect on Contribution Gap of Reduction In Replacement Rate by 5 Percentage Points	
		New pensioners only	All pensioners
Major industrial countries	1.8	−0.7	−1.1
United States	0.8	−0.7	−1.2
Japan	3.3	−0.5	−0.7
Germany	3.4	−1.2	−1.4
France	3.3	−0.9	−1.3
Italy	2.5	−0.7	−0.8
United Kingdom	0.1	−0.7	−0.8
Canada	2.0	−1.0	−1.2
Sweden	0.9	−1.0	−1.2

Source: IMF staff estimates.

generations of pensioners. Insofar as the latter are currently working, they are in effect being presented with the choice of either higher contribution rates now or lower future benefits. The debates have often ranged over various alternatives without any clear resolution in many cases.

The discussion that follows focuses on reforms that involve lowering benefits and extending retirement ages, taking account of the politically important distinction between future or new pensioners and existing pensioners. The technique for assessing the various options that are considered here is to examine their impact on the sustainable contribution gaps that were presented in the preceding section.

Reducing Average Replacement Rates

The first option to be considered is that of reducing the average replacement rate by way of a discontinuous adjustment, thereby lowering in one step the benefits enjoyed by pensioners as a proportion of average wages. A distinction is drawn between "new" or "all" pensioners (the latter including existing ones as well). One way of lowering the replacement ratio would be to reduce accrual factors; another would be to increase the number of years of income used for determining the average income level upon which the accrual factors would apply; a third would combine both approaches. A fairly drastic adjustment would be to reduce the replacement rate by, say, 5 percentage points, the illustrative experiment considered here. The severity of this measure would of course vary with the initial level of the replacement rate,

amounting, for example, to a 10 percent reduction if the replacement rate were initially set at 50 percent.

The last column of Table 12 shows the effects of such a change on the baseline contribution gap, when all pensioners, current and future, are subject to the lower replacement rates. Substantial improvements in contribution gaps are obtained, ranging from full elimination of the gap for the United States, the United Kingdom, and Sweden to a reduction of the gap by about one fourth to one half for all the other countries. Of course, for existing pensioners a reduction in the replacement rate would imply an immediate reduction in income levels and thus would obviously be perceived as grossly unfair. Nevertheless, restricting the adjustment to new pensioners shows that even here there are significant gains to be had. In the case of Germany, for example, about one third of the contribution gap is eliminated, only a little less than if all pensioners were affected.

Modifying Indexation Provisions

Another approach to reducing replacement rates is to modify indexation provisions. While indexing to nominal wages will essentially preserve the gross replacement rate,[31] few industrial countries have adopted this approach. Since only Germany, Japan, and France (in part) of the countries enumerated in

---

[31]However, if the replacement rate is indexed to nominal gross wages, retirees will do better than when it is indexed to net wages in periods during which contribution rates and income taxes are raised.

Table 13. Effect of Different Indexation Schemes on Contribution Gaps
(In percent of GDP)

	Baseline Projection	Effect on Baseline of:	
		100 percent CPI indexation	80 percent CPI indexation
Major industrial countries	1.8	−0.5	−0.8
United States	0.8	—	−0.2
Japan	3.3	−1.4	−1.5
Germany	3.4	−1.9	−2.3
France	3.3	−0.8	−1.4
Italy	2.5	—	−0.2
United Kingdom	0.1	—	−0.5
Canada	2.0	—	−0.4
Sweden	0.9	—	−0.6

Source: IMF staff estimates.

Table 13 index pensions to wages, these are the only countries that would obtain savings from a move to 100 percent CPI indexation. Some additional gains would be obtained if indexation was to be less than 100 percent, say 80 percent.[32] However, the additional gains of partial CPI indexation are, at the projected 3 percent steady-state inflation rate, not that large, even though the relative income position of pensioners compared with wage earners would deteriorate over time.

With positive labor productivity growth, CPI indexation leads to an erosion of replacement rates over the lifetime of a pensioner. To illustrate, Table 14 shows the percentage amounts by which replacement rates would decline for different growth rates of labor productivity when pensions are fully indexed to the cost of living index. The longer the retirement span, or the higher the rate of labor productivity growth, the bigger the decrease in replacement rates. For example, at the baseline labor productivity growth rate of 1.5 percent and a retirement span of 20 years, a pensioner's replacement rate would be compressed by almost 26 percent. An interesting trade-off is posed for those countries indexing to nominal net wages such as Germany and Japan, because they can choose between an initial one-shot reduction in replacement rates while continuing to retain wage indexation, or what is broadly equivalent in terms of impacts on contribution gaps, they can allow for a gradual decline in replacement rates by moving to CPI indexation.

[32]At a projected annual inflation rate of 3 percent, this would reduce CPI indexation by 0.6 percentage point. Partial CPI indexation could be motivated as an offset to upward bias of the CPI as a measure of living costs. Recent estimates put the upward bias in the U.S. CPI at about 1 percentage point.

Extending Retirement Ages

Another option frequently considered is to delay the age at which a worker becomes eligible for a pension.[33] This has been undertaken by several countries, most notably the United States, which will gradually extend the normal retirement age at which a full pension is received for both men and women to 67 years. Table 15 presents some estimates of the effects of extending retirement ages on contribution gaps. Preannounced increases in retirement ages have already been taken into account in the projections that were presented in the previous chapter. To explore the impact of a more radical option, the question is posed of what the effects of the preannounced measures would be if they were implemented immediately in 1995. The results are shown in column 2 of Table 15. They indicate significant effects on contribution gaps, particularly for Italy.

The next question asked is that of the effects on sustainable contribution rates if retirement ages were immediately to be extended to 67 for both men and women. As is evident from the last column, the effects can be sizable, especially for those countries, such as France and Italy, for whom retirement ages

[33]To be effective and, at the same time, permit the choice of withdrawing from the labor market before reaching the statutory retirement age, such a policy would need to be combined with flexible retirement arrangements that provide appropriate disincentives to limit early retirement. Industrial country experience indicates a sharply rising trend in the rate of early retirement, which may to some extent have been driven by the deterioration in the overall employment situation but may also reflect increased demand for lifetime leisure given rising income levels. Disincentives to early retirement would certainly include a reduction in pension accrual factors, reflecting the actuarially higher costs of receiving a pension over a longer time span.

Table 14. Effect of CPI Indexation on Pension Replacement Rates: Illustrative Examples

(In percent)

Years Spent in Retirement	Labor Productivity Growth During Retirement (In percent per year)		
	1.0	1.5	2.5
10 years	−9.9	−13.8	−21.9
15 years	−13.9	−20.0	−30.9
20 years	−18.0	−25.7	−39.0

Source: IMF staff estimates.

Note: The table shows the percentage point reduction in the pension replacement rate for different retirement spans and for different growth rates of labor productivity if pensions are indexed to the CPI inflation rate. For example, the replacement rate of a pension with a retirement span of 15 years will decrease by 20 percent if labor productivity grows by 1.5 percent.

higher proportional cost of such reforms to women should also be noted, particularly in Italy and Japan (where the present retirement ages of women are 57 and 55 years, respectively) and France and the United Kingdom (where it is presently 60).

Mix of Reforms

The above review of likely effects of major parametric reforms shows considerable scope for eliminating contribution gaps without altering the fundamental structure of the existing public pension systems, although this varies with the country. The underlying nature of the pension arrangements for the country, together with the severity of projected demographic factors, and, of course, considerations of equity and political feasibility, would obviously be factors influencing the approach to reform. For the United States, the United Kingdom, and Sweden, relatively small increases in current average contribution rates might suffice, provided these are sustained over the projection period. A moderate reduction in the replacement ratio for the United States might also be possible, although apparently much less so for the United Kingdom and Sweden, whose replacement rates are already projected to decline sharply over the projection period.

For Germany, France, and Italy, for whom contribution rates are already very high, there is probably greater scope for adjustment through reducing high replacement rates and, especially for France and Italy, extending retirement ages. While the last alone could suffice for Italy, some small increases in contribution rates may in addition be unavoidable for Germany. This is also likely to be the case for Japan,

are well below 67. In fact, for Italy, the baseline contribution gap is more than wiped out as is the case for Sweden and the United Kingdom. For the major industrial countries more than two thirds of the contribution gap would be eliminated by extending retirement ages immediately to 67. Again, a gradual phasing in of reforms would clearly be necessary, in order to limit the perceived unfairness to workers close to retirement, who would have only limited opportunity to make the requisite financial adjustment in their consumption and savings behavior. The

Table 15. Effect of Changes in Retirement Ages on Contribution Gaps

(In percent of GDP)

	Baseline Projection	Effect on Baseline Projection of	
		Front loading of announced retirement age increases	Unified retirement ages at 67 years in 1995
Major industrial countries	1.8	−0.5	−1.4
United States	0.8	−0.3	−0.3
Japan	3.3	−0.8	−1.6
Germany	3.4	−0.4	−1.2
France	3.3	−0.4	−3.7
Italy	2.5	−1.1	−5.7
United Kingdom	0.1	−0.4	−1.1
Canada	2.0	—	−0.7
Sweden	0.9	—	−1.0

Source: IMF staff estimates.

for whom an initial small but sustained increase in contribution rates, combined with a move to cost of living indexation and an increase in retirement ages, should be sufficient to stabilize the system.

Systemic Reforms of Defined-Contribution Type

While the above reforms could lead to financial equilibrium under a PAYG system, they may raise several concerns among policymakers. One concern is that the reforms will result in contribution rates that are higher than current contribution rates or lead to excessive cutbacks in future benefit levels. A related concern is the further erosion of the perceived implicit return, in the form of future pension benefits, associated with higher payroll tax contributions by workers.

Some critics of the existing system have argued that more fundamental changes are needed that could address both concerns. Taking note of the widespread implementation of defined-contribution schemes in the private sector, they have argued for a shift toward a similar approach in the public pension system. The experiences of Singapore and Chile have drawn considerable attention: the former initiated a compulsary saving scheme to finance retirement incomes in 1955, and the latter shifted to a fully funded defined contribution type of system in the early 1980s. Many feel that a major attraction of the fully funded scheme is that it more directly links the mandatory contributions on behalf of an individual to the pensionable benefits that the worker ultimately receives.

Shifting to a Defined-Contribution System

For industrial countries two aspects of the defined-contribution approach that may be of particular appeal are (1) its potential reduction in the distortion of labor market behavior reputedly associated with payroll taxation under the PAYG approach, an issue of particular concern in a number of European countries, and (2) the seeming avoidance of large fiscal costs associated with the aging process. For some countries, an additional appealing feature could be the Chilean approach of investing the accumulated assets of such funds in a diversified portfolio of assets at the discretion of contributors themselves. This increase in transparency and control could reduce the real or perceived risk of the government's exploiting a large captive source of funds, thereby increasing the rate of return.

As against these advantages that have been put forward, a number of complications are likely for industrial countries. The management of the Chilean system has proved to be very costly and appears to far exceed the administrative costs of managing a defined-benefit, PAYG system. In addition, the adequacy of pension benefits under such systems has yet to be fully demonstrated against the standards applied in industrial countries. Rates of return on accumulated contributions in Chile have been relatively high—a condition that may not always be duplicated in industrial countries. The defined-contribution scheme has also been faulted for being unable adequately to insure households against shocks to longevity, earnings, and inflation, unlike the PAYG Scheme. A critical issue associated with systemic reform involving a substitution of a defined-contribution system for a PAYG structure has to do with fiscal transition costs. These are likely to be especially high for industrial countries with well-developed public pension systems.

If a government attempts to move from an extant PAYG scheme to a new defined-contribution, fully funded system, the essence of the reform would involve institutional changes. Pension benefits to existing pensioners, under the defined-benefit system, would continue to be the responsibility of the government (or of the former pension institutions). Yet contributions of some (to be determined) component of the labor force would be channeled, not for the financing of these pension outlays, but for investment into some form of pension-related, individually linked savings accounts. Thus, the government would be faced with the obligation of having to meet continuing pension liabilities for what may be a lengthy period, but without the "offsetting" flow of payroll tax contributions. As discussed below, the size of the deficits that would emerge under the PAYG system would depend on how quickly the fully funded schemes are introduced.

Transition Costs

Two alternative scenarios are considered here: (1) a gradual transition under which only new entrants to the labor force would be required to join the fully funded defined-contribution scheme, and (2) a sudden transition, that would require all current and future beneficiaries to shift to a fully funded system.[34] It might be noted that the moment a move to a fully funded system is contemplated, it would be necessary to make explicit the gross liabilities of the public pension system, which is undertaken next.

---

[34]An aspect not explicitly examined here concerns possible additional costs that may be encountered to induce participants of a PAYG scheme to opt for a fully funded scheme, if the choice is not mandated. A tax concession, such as allowing contributions to be deducted under the income tax, might be required to weight the choice in favor of the fully funded system.

Table 16. Decomposition of Gross Liabilities of Public Pension Systems, 1995–2050

(In percent of 1995 GDP)

	Gross Pension Liability	=	Pension Liability Present Retirees	+	Pension Liability Present Workforce	+	Pension Liability Due to New Rights
Major industrial countries	288.9		65.1		95.6		...
United States	206.1		31.7		76.6		97.8
Japan	261.1		67.7		98.0		95.4
Germany	456.5		106.2		114.7		235.6
France	523.2		128.2		136.4		258.6
Italy	559.5		170.8		186.6		202.1
United Kingdom	148.1		44.8		71.8		31.4
Canada[1]	213.8		43.7		49.9		...
Sweden[1]	291.4		52.9		78.1		...

Source: IMF staff estimates.

[1]Pension liabilities for present retirees and workforce include only earnings-related pension schemes.

Table 16 decomposes the present values of the gross liabilities of the PAYG system over the projection period. The gross pension liabilities are broken down into three parts—those of present retirees, those attributable to the present workforce, and those that will accrue to future generations of workers if the present system were continued. Gross pension liabilities of the major industrial countries are estimated at nearly three times their collective GDP, of which one third is accounted for by the present workforce. These liabilities and the associated contributions for each of the three groups considered are the basic building blocks needed to assess the fiscal costs of a shift to a new type of pension regime.

Gradual Transition

In a gradual transition to a fully funded system, under which only new entrants would be switched to the new system, the government would continue to receive contributions from members of the current workforce. These will taper away as current members retire, eventually disappearing altogether at which time the workforce would comprise only workers who subscribe to the fully funded, defined-contribution system. During part of the transition, the numbers of current pensioners would rise, while contributions would fall, giving rise to a growing deficit on the social security accounts. The accumulation of these deficits would increase the government's net pension liabilities. Eventually, as the last eligible pensioner dies off, the government would no longer be paying any pension benefits and would be

in a state of equilibrium, except for the need to service the accumulated net liabilities.

Initially, the fully funded system would be building up financial reserves, as only contributions flow in; this would continue until the first new entrant into the labor force retires and is eligible to cash his accumulated contributions with interest and convert them into an annuity. Table 17 shows, in present value terms, the resulting net liabilities for the public sector and the fully funded system, with the latter viewed as outside the public sector. In all cases, the public sector is left with a large net pension liability, in several cases a multiple of the net pension liability under the present PAYG system. Given the macroeconomic assumptions regarding the real interest rate and inflation rates, most countries would be subject to a nominal interest rate of some 7 percent. Meeting this interest charge would increase fiscal deficits by substantial amounts, ranging from an additional 1 percent of GDP for Japan to some 6 percent of GDP for Germany. The fully funded system would, however, be earning substantial amounts of net interest income or its equivalent.

Sudden Transition

If instead a sudden transition is made to the fully funded system, the government would be deprived of the contributions of current members of the workforce. All participants of the public pension scheme would be "cashed out" by having their accrued rights recognized and transferred to the fully funded system. The government would be left with greater

Table 17. Fiscal Implications of a Gradual Transition to a Fully Funded System, 1995–2050
(In percent of 1995 GDP)

	Net Pension Liability Present Arrangements	Net Pension Liabilities Under Gradual Reform		
		Public sector system	Fully funded system	Consolidated pension system
Major industrial countries	60.0	125.8	−65.8	60.0
United States	25.7	95.7	−70.0	25.7
Japan	106.8	137.9	−31.0	106.9
Germany	110.7	205.3	−94.6	110.7
France	113.6	242.6	−129.0	113.6
Italy	75.5	126.6	−51.1	75.5
United Kingdom	4.6	61.9	−57.3	4.6
Canada	67.8	87.0	−19.2	67.8
Sweden	20.4	84.4	−64.0	20.4

Source: IMF staff estimates.

liabilities than under gradual transition, as is indicated by a comparison of column 2 in Tables 17 and 18.[35] For the major industrial countries, net pension liabilities under a sudden transition would be some 25 percentage points of GDP higher than under the more gradual transition, which in turn would be about twice that under present PAYG arrangements. Correspondingly, the net assets of the fully funded system would be larger than under a gradual transition. Interestingly, the net liability position of the consolidated system is substantially smaller than under gradual transition, which in turn is identical to that under present arrangements, given that the full effects of the gradual transition are not manifested until well beyond the projection horizon of 2050. In terms of reducing the net liabilities of the consolidated system and rendering the pension system more self-sustaining in the face of population aging, the sudden transition is clearly preferred. However, a gradual transition may be politically more acceptable; furthermore, at least in the government's eyes, it has the advantage of lower fiscal costs.

Restructured Defined-Benefit System

As against the alternatives of a PAYG and a defined-contribution scheme, a more appealing alter-

---

[35]For Canada and Sweden, the net pension liabilities under sudden reform include only liabilities of the earnings-related schemes (and exclude liabilities related to the flat-rate schemes); for these countries, the results in Tables 17 and 18 are not comparable.

native could be to combine features of both. The postwar experience of the industrial countries has illustrated the problems that can arise with a PAYG system both as it matures and as the population ages. In the initial years of a PAYG scheme, relatively low contribution rates were usually more than adequate to cover benefit payments. Over time as the population began to age and the proportion of retirees increased, the initial contribution rates proved inadequate, but given that they were low to begin with, it was generally feasible to raise them. Eventually, however, there was less scope for further increases in pension-related contribution rates.

In principle, the problem of having continually to raise contribution rates to preserve benefits could have been avoided had there been sufficient foresight. By anticipating future demands, for example, as the United States did in 1983, a sustainable contribution rate could have been selected that would then have been maintained for the long run. Owing to uncertainties about the timing and extent of future demographic changes, a conservative policy would be to err on the high side in setting payroll tax rates. The essence of the farsighted approach is to build up a reserve fund during the initial years, when the flow of contributions exceeds benefits paid out, which can then be drawn down as the population ages.

Accumulating a reserve fund may also be economically advantageous. As already noted, a steep rise in elderly dependency ratios in industrial countries appears inevitable, with the implication that a greater share of national output will be transferred to the retired. However, the impact of that transfer on

Table 18. Fiscal Implications of a Sudden Transition to a Fully Funded System, 1995–2050
(In percent of 1995 GDP)

	Net Pension Liability Present Arrangements	Net Pension Liabilities Under Sudden Reform		
		Public sector system	Fully funded system	Consolidated pension system
Major industrial countries	60.0	151.8	−117.9	...
United States	25.7	101.7	−75.8	22.9
Japan	106.8	140.3	−77.3	63.0
Germany	110.7	219.9	−174.9	45.0
France	113.6	264.5	−221.4	43.1
Italy	75.5	357.4	−335.5	21.9
United Kingdom	4.6	116.7	−73.1	43.6
Canada[1]	67.8	62.8	−111.8	...
Sweden[1]	20.4	105.1	−99.3	...

Source: IMF staff estimates.

[1]Net pension liabilities of public sector system under sudden reform scenario include only earnings-related schemes.

workers would be mitigated to the extent that output per worker increases over time. In that context, it has been argued that the accumulation of social security reserves would result in an increase in national savings and an associated higher path of capital accumulation and hence output. Reserve funding may have the further advantage of strengthening financial discipline if the publication of regular reports on the actuarial status of the reserve fund heightens awareness of the future cost implications of today's pension benefit promises.

However, the reserve fund approach, notably including its implications for national savings, is not without controversy. First, suppose that, as in the United States, the reserve fund surpluses count towards overall fiscal deficit targets. Insofar as policymakers frame nonpension tax and expenditure proposals with an eye on the overall fiscal deficit, the consolidated fiscal position of government and, as a consequence, national savings may not improve by much. Moreover, this outcome could have the distributional consequence of financing an expansion of government activities by an increase in regressive payroll taxes. In a later period, when, as a consequence of aging, benefits paid out exceed contributions, and the pension fund is being depleted, keeping the consolidated fiscal position unchanged will require an offsetting move into surplus by the rest of government. This could necessitate disruptive increases in general taxes or cutbacks in expenditure. The extent to which the accumulation of reserve fund surpluses leads to offsetting government

behavior may importantly depend on the stability and discipline of budgetary institutions. In this context, it has been argued that formally excluding reserve fund surpluses from overall fiscal targets provides some assurance against misuse of pension fund reserves.[36]

Second, even if the surpluses of the reserve fund are not being siphoned away by a bigger non-pension fiscal deficit, an equivalent increase in national savings may not occur. One possibility is that there would be a full offsetting decline in private savings.[37] The more likely outcome would be a partial offset by private savings reflecting, for example, the prevalence of liquidity constraints. In such circumstances, and assuming unchanged pension benefits, the consumption possibilities of the future retired generation will be curtailed while those of the new contributing generations will have benefited as their sustainable contribution rate will now be lower than

[36]See, for example, Munnell and Ernsberger (1990). They also review the experiences with social security reserve fund surpluses and national savings in Japan, Canada, and Sweden, concluding in particular that both Japan and Sweden apparently increased government savings by building up social security reserves, while Canada probably did not.

[37]Potential reasons for such an offsetting decline in private savings include a reduction in uncertainty concerning future benefits following the implementation of a credible reform package and the current generation reacting to the increase in contribution rates so as to maintain unchanged lifetime consumption possibilities across generations. In the literature, this latter possibility is often referred to as Ricardian equivalence.

the higher equilibrium rate of the standard PAYG system.[38]

A third issue concerns the management of the fund, and in particular the choice between investment in government securities and equities. On the face of it, replacing the customary investment in government securities with private equities, on which higher returns are generally obtained, should help reduce the burden on the contributing generations. However, by investing funds in equity markets, the reserve fund would also be exposed to additional risk. It may be contended that the return advantage of investment in private equities is spurious. The argument is that a shift in pension fund portfolios in favor of private equities will affect market prices, reducing yields on equity but raising bond interest rates. The latter implies higher deb-service charges, which would necessitate tax increases to keep the fiscal deficit unchanged, assuming that the government maintains a firm fiscal target. Indeed, the outcome could be one where the private sector suffers relative to the public sector: the increased flow of debt-service receipts is offset by higher taxes, while equity incomes would be lower. As a result the overall rate of return to private saving declines, with obvious adverse effects. However, it could also be argued that such a portfolio shift, by lowering the cost of equity capital, stimulates capital accumulation and increases future output levels. This should make the pension-related burden easier to bear.

Cost of Alternative Reforms

The earlier discussion indicated the large fiscal burden that would be imposed on a government if it moves to a fully funded scheme (Tables 17 and 18). There is also the issue of how the sizable debt burdens would now be financed. The latter issue, insofar as it concerns stocks, can be quickly disposed of as the government's explicit debt recognition would not be immediately called in under a gradual transition, whereas under a sudden transition, such debt would most likely be purchased by investment funds established under a fully funded system, provided a market-related return is paid. Servicing of the debt may, however, raise problems. For several of the countries, this debt service would be sufficiently large as to add several percentage points to the fiscal deficit to GDP ratio. This raises the issue that meeting a sizable interest burden on the recognized accumulated pension liabilities in perpetuity may require addi-

tional fiscal adjustments of a size comparable to that needed to stabilize existing PAYG arrangements.

Table 19 presents results comparing the adjustments needed in primary balances to preserve overall fiscal sustainability under present arrangements and under the two approaches to a fully funded system. As is to be expected in light of the substantial increase in the liabilities of the public sector generated by the move to a fully funded system (outside the public sector), the primary balance adjustments needed are higher. For example, for the major industrial countries as a group, the required permanent increase in primary balances is about 2 percent of GDP under gradual transition. However, as is indicated in Table 8, the permanent improvement in primary balances needed to prevent a buildup of pension debt for the group of major industrial countries is also about 2 percent of GDP. This result illustrates the so-called double payment problem of moving to a private fully funded pension system, but also suggests that it may be significantly less costly to fix the present public pension system, depending on the country's specific situation and preferences. For certain of the countries the issue may be moot; for example, for Germany, fixing the present public pension system requires a permanent improvement in the primary balance of 3.4 percent of GDP (Table 8), whereas the additional cost of moving gradually to a fully funded system is about 3 percent of GDP.

When comparing the fiscal cost of alternative reform options, note should also be taken of potential fiscal savings that may accrue beyond the cutoff year 2050. In the case of the transition to a fully funded system, it may be argued that beyond 2050 the public sector would be relieved of the burden of running a large pension system. By contrast, if the public pension system is preserved, additional increases in contributions or cuts in benefits may be needed to maintain fiscal sustainability beyond 2050. At the same time, the transition to a fully funded pension system is unlikely to relieve the public sector of all pension-related fiscal burdens as at least a redistributive pillar would need to be financed from general taxation.

For those countries for whom fixing the present public pension system is the preferred course of action, the outcome would be a sustainable contribution rate, the level of which would depend on the benefit adjustments undertaken. Nevertheless, the issue remains of how to deal with a pension-related crisis that originates from a lack of foresight and the dissipation of contributions that were received, possibly compounded by the provision of excessive benefits. A solution might be to generate some fiscal savings that could be applied to restoring the financial viability of the public pension scheme. As noted earlier, one avenue would be to engage in asset sales,

---

[38]This line of reasoning also assumes that the current generation's bequest behavior would be unaffected by the reform, a likely outcome if most individuals are liquidity constrained.

Table 19. Sustainable Fiscal Stance Under Different Systemic Pension Reform Options, 1995–2050
(In percent of GDP)

	Permanent Primary Balance Adjustment in 1995 Needed to Preserve Fiscal Sustainability in Case of		
	Maintaining present public sector system[1] (1)	Gradual transition to fully funded system[2] (2)	Sudden transition to fully funded system[3] (3)
Major industrial countries	2.2	4.1	...
United States	1.5	3.4	3.6
Japan	3.8	4.7	4.8
Germany	2.1	4.9	5.3
France	4.3	8.1	8.8
Italy	1.3	3.1	11.3
United Kingdom	0.4	2.1	3.7
Canada[4]	4.5	5.1	...
Sweden[4]	6.1	8.3	...

Source: IMF staff estimates.

[1]Corresponds to column (7) in Table 8.

[2]Defined as column (1) plus increase in primary balance needed to prevent additional buildup of debt due to gradual transition to fully funded system.

[3]Defined as column (1) plus increase in primary balance needed to prevent additional buildup of debt due to sudden transition to fully funded system.

[4]Net pension liabilities of public sector system under sudden reform scenario include only earnings-related schemes.

or alternatively there could be scope for general expenditure cuts and even some revenue increases. However, if the preceding resolutions are inadequate, it might be necessary to reconsider some of the parametric reforms of the pension system that were examined earlier. It could be noted that insofar as the pension problem originates from an extension of life expectancies that may not have been adequately anticipated, there is a natural merit in extending retirement ages and discouraging earlier retirement.

V Conclusions

This study set out to examine the fiscal implications of population aging in the context of present public pension arrangements, with particular reference to the major industrial countries. While population aging is a widespread phenomenon, it is particularly pronounced in the industrial countries. The study confirms that under the existing public pension arrangements, which rely heavily on PAYG schemes, the aging of the population has started to contribute to serious fiscal stresses in most of the major industrial countries, and that these are likely to get much worse over the next few decades in the absence of appropriate reforms. The study finds that different countries are not all identically placed with respect to the severity of the potential crises, depending in large part on their pension arrangements. Nevertheless, as a group, the industrial countries face daunting deficits and the prospect of heavy debt accumulations that in the absence of policy adjustments could adversely impact on global financial flows and interest rates.

Fortunately, there is still a window of opportunity for most of the industrial countries, as the full impact of the aging problem is not likely to be felt for another 15 years or so. However, reform actions will have to be initiated soon, both because the lead time for changing pension arrangements is likely to be long and because sizable costs can be avoided, the earlier the adjustment. Growing recognition of the potentially adverse implications of the aging problem and of the limited time available for satisfactorily addressing the problem has triggered widespread discussions on pension reform, but it is, in many instances, proving painfully difficult to obtain a satisfactory consensus. Aside from a clear understanding and analysis of the economic, distributional, and administrative implications of the different reform proposals, which a review of the debates does not always reveal, considerable political acumen and a willingness to compromise will be needed to mediate between the different entrenched interests.

In the calculus set out in the study for assessing the effects of parametric reforms that modify existing pension arrangements, considerable scope is found, depending on the underlying pension arrangements in the country and the extent of aging, for adjustments involving both contributions and benefit structures, but especially the latter, for addressing the looming fiscal problems. One procedure that has merit is to extend the retirement age, combined with greater economic disincentives to earlier retirement, as a way of directly containing the effects of aging. Another, which has the appealing feature that it preserves the level of pensions relative to the past real incomes of the beneficiaries is to index pensions to the CPI. This is least problematic if future per capita real incomes grow very slowly as the relative standing of pensioners will not deteriorate much. However, if per capita real incomes are growing, there may be pressure to index pensions to wages. In that event, an alternative approach, which takes some account of the uncertainties that characterize the future, especially with regard to demographic projections and macroeconomic assumptions, is to index benefits to net wages (net of contributions) as in Germany and Japan. Such an approach ensures that pensioners share some of the burden that would arise if rising contribution rates slowed the growth of net wages. In all these cases, it would be desirable to build up a substantial pension reserve fund that could be drawn upon when needed to take account of demographic and other contingencies.

More generally, it is advisable to introduce a sustainable contribution rate that takes adequate account of future aging. The size of the sustainable rate will depend on the nature of the benefit reforms. It is conceivable that if the sustainable rate is introduced early and benefit reforms are sufficient, the sustainable rate could be lower than present contribution rates. Not least of the advantages of introducing a constant sustainable rate are its equity features—different generations are subject to the same proportional contribution rate.

This study has also examined the fiscal consequences of introducing a fully funded scheme system in place of the defined-benefit PAYG system. It finds that the fiscal costs of undertaking such a shift may be very high, and that meeting these costs may require, in many cases, an amount of fiscal adjustment that is substantially higher than what would be needed to fix the PAYG system. While there are several advantages to the PAYG system, not least of which are that it involves a compact between the generations, avoids start-up delays in extending pension benefits to prospective and current retirees, and insures against several major sources of risk, the system is particularly vulnerable to the aging phenome-non, unlike the more individual-based, defined-contribution, fully funded schemes. However, as we have noted, it is possible to place the defined-benefit system on a satisfactory long-term footing. This course of action would require anticipating the demands associated with aging through implementing a constant sustainable contribution rate.

Appendix I   Analytical Framework and Data Sources for Public Pension Projections

This appendix describes the model and data sources underlying the projections of public pension finances in the selected industrial countries covered by the study.

Asset Position and Balance

The asset position (A_t) of the public pension fund evolves as

$$A_t = (1 + R_t)A_{t-1} + C_t - P_t, \qquad (1)$$

where C_t denotes public pension fund revenue including budget transfers, P_t is public pension expenditure including administrative costs, and R_t is the nominal interest rate on assets. Expressing (1) in percent of nominal GDP and denoting the growth rate of nominal GDP by g_t gives

$$a_t = [(1 + R_t)/(1 + g_t)]a_{t-1} + c_t - p_t, \qquad (1)'$$

where a_t, c_t, and p_t denote variables expressed as a percent of nominal GDP.

To bring out the fiscal implications of population aging, the model views the public pension system as a single fund, which is separated from other elements of general government operations. The purpose of the model is to project pension fund revenue (C_t) and expenditure (P_t) given projections for demographic and macroeconomic developments and assumptions for the characteristics of the public pension system. The time horizon for the projections is 1995–2050.

Projection of Revenue

Revenue of the public pension fund is defined as the sum of pension contributions of insured workers (C_{1t}) and net transfers from other budgets (C_{2t}):

$$C_t = C_{1t} + C_{2t}. \qquad (2)$$

If strict pay-as-you-go principles apply, the asset position of the fund would be zero in all time periods. However, for the purposes of the projections, pension fund revenue is assumed to grow at about the same rate as nominal GDP. In particular, revenue is projected as follows. First, net transfers to the public pension fund (C_{2t}) are kept constant as a percent of nominal GDP at their 1994 value. Second, projected pension contributions of insured workers (C_{1t}) are derived from

$$C_{1t} = \sum_{s=m,f} \sum_{k=1}^{n} NC_t^{s,k} \, W_t^{s,k} \, \phi_t, \qquad (3)$$

where $NC_t^{s,k}$ is the number of contributors of sex s and age k, $W_t^{s,k}$ is the average gross wage of contributors of sex s and age k, and ϕ_t is the effective average contribution rate, assumed to be invariant across cohorts and across time. The number of contributors of sex s and age k is calculated as

$$NC_t^{s,k} = POP_t^{s,k} \, LFP_t^{s,k} \, (1 - U_t^{s,k})INS_t^{s,k}, \qquad (4)$$

where $POP_t^{s,k}$ is the number of members of population cohort of sex s and age k, $LFP_t^{s,k}$ is the cohort-specific labor force participation rate, $U_t^{s,k}$ is the cohort-specific unemployment rate, and $INS_t^{s,k}$ is the cohort-specific share of persons contributing to the public pension fund.

Projection of Expenditure

Pension fund expenditure in a given year is the sum of expenditure for pensioners who retired during the given year (P_{1t}) ("new pensioners") and expenditure for pensioners who retired during previous years (P_{2t}) ("pre-existing pensioners"):

$$P_t = P_{1t} + P_{2t}. \qquad (5)$$

Pension expenditure for new and pre-existing pensioners are defined as

$$P_{it} = \sum_{s=m,f} \sum_{k=1}^{n} NB_{it}^{s,k} \, PB_{it}^{s,k}, \qquad i = 1,2 \qquad (6)$$

where $NB_{it}^{s,k}$ is the number of new and pre-existing retirees of sex s and age k, respectively, and $PB_{it}^{s,k}$ is the average pension benefit of new and pre-existing retirees of sex s and age k, respectively. The number of new and pre-existing beneficiaries is given by

$$NB_{it}^{s,k} = POP_i^{s,k} \, EL_{it}^{s,k}, \qquad i = 1,2 \qquad (7)$$

where $EL_{it}^{s,k}$ is the share of new and pre-existing pensioners of cohort of sex s and age k, respectively. The average pension benefit of new pensioners of sex s and age k is usually a function of the earnings history of contributors, but the exact benefit formula may differ across countries. For example, in the specific case of Germany, the average pension benefit of a new pensioner is calculated using the formula

$$PB_{1t}^{s,k} = PV_t \sum_{j=0}^{q^{s,k}} (W_{t-j}^{s,k}/W_{t-j}),$$

where PV_t is the "pension value" in year t, and $q^{s,k}$ is the average length of the earnings history of new pensioners of sex s and age k. The average pension benefit of pre-existing pensioners depends on the pension indexation arrangements in place.

Projection of Macroeconomic Variables

For the period 1995–99, projections of macroeconomic variables are generally based on May 1995 *World Economic Outlook* projections. For 2000–50, the real rate of interest (r_t) and the inflation rate (π_t) in all countries are exogenously fixed at 3.5 percent and 3 percent, respectively, and the nominal interest rate is given by

$$R_t = [(1 + r_t)(1 + \pi_t)] - 1. \qquad (8)$$

The growth rate of real GDP during 2000–50 reflects a Cobb-Douglas production function with labor-augmenting technical progress:

$$Y_t = K_t^{\alpha} E_t^{1-\alpha}, \qquad (9)$$

where Y_t is real GDP, K_t is the capital stock, and E_t is labor input measured in effective units. From (9), real GDP growth is given by

$$(\Delta Y_t/Y_t) = \alpha(\Delta K_t/K_t) + (1 - \alpha)(\Delta E_t/E_t). \qquad (10)$$

Labor-augmenting technical progress in all countries is assumed to occur at a constant rate λ (1.5 percent) while labor input (employment) grows at rate n_t.[39] The growth rate of employment is derived from exogenous assumptions about gender- and age-specific labor force participation and unemployment rates, which are kept constant for each cohort throughout the projection period. As a consequence, overall labor force participation and unemployment rates may change as the demographic composition of the population changes. Labor input growth in the

Cobb-Douglas production function measured in effective units is equal to the growth rate of employment plus the rate of labor-augmenting technical progress. Thus, defining steady state as balanced growth of the capital stock and effective labor input, real GDP in steady state would grow at the rate $\lambda + n$.

Nominal gross wage growth equals the inflation rate plus labor productivity growth ($\pi_t + \lambda$), an assumption assuring a constant labor share over the projection period.

Projection of Demographic Variables

Data on future population trends, required to calculate the number of contributors and beneficiaries in equations (4) and (7), respectively, are taken from the World Bank's *World Population Projections, 1994–95* by Bos and others (1994).

Indicators of the Fiscal Position

Using (1)', the asset position of the public pension fund in any future time period $t + n$ can be written as

$$a_{t+n} = (\prod_{j=0}^{n} d_{t+j})a_{t-1} + \sum_{j=0}^{n} (\prod_{k=j+1}^{n} d_{t+k})[c_{t+j} - p_{t+j}], \quad (11)$$

where the discount factors are defined as $d_{t+j} = [(1 + R_{t+j})/(1 + g_{t+j})]$. The present value of the fund's primary balances between t and $t + n$ minus the net asset position at t represents an estimate of the net pension liability of the fund expressed as a percent of GDP in period t. Using equation (11), the net pension liability is

$$a_{t,n}^* = a_{t+n}/(\prod_{j=1}^{n} d_{t+j}), \qquad (12)$$

where the notation $a_{t,n}^*$ indicates that the net pension liability is evaluated at the beginning of the projection period and that it depends on the length of the projection period as captured by the parameter n.

An alternative indicator of the fiscal position of the public pension fund can be calculated by requiring sustainability of the public pension fund over the projection period. Sustainability of a fiscal position is defined as a setting of expenditure and revenue flows such that the net liability position at the end of the projection horizon (a_{t+n}) is equal to the initial net liability position (a_{t-1}).[40] It is convenient to express the sustainability requirement as the constant amount of yearly contributions (including budget

---

[39]In the case of Germany, it is assumed that during 2000–10 labor-augmenting technical progress grows at a rate sufficient to ensure convergence—by 2010—of labor productivity per employee in east Germany to west German levels.

[40]See Blanchard and others (1990) for an analytical discussion of the concept of sustainability of fiscal policy.

transfers) as a percent of GDP (c_t^*) needed to pre-serve the sustainability of the fund. Setting $a_{t+n} = a_{t-1}$ in (11), and replacing c_{t+j} by the constant effective contribution ratio c_t^* yields the expression

$$c_{t,n}^* = [(1 - \prod_{j=0}^{n} d_{t+j})a_{t-1} + \sum_{j=0}^{n} (\prod_{k=j+1}^{n} d_{t+k}) p_{t+j}]/$$

$$\sum_{j=0}^{n} (\prod_{k=j+1}^{n} d_{t+k}). \qquad (13)$$

The value of the constant contribution rate $c_{t,n}^*$ can be compared with the actual contribution rate to in-dicate the adjustment in fiscal stance needed to pre-serve sustainability of the public pension fund. The difference between the sustainable contribution rate and the contribution rate in t defines the contribution gap ($c_{t,n}^* - c_t$).

Pension reforms affect expenditure and revenue flows of the fund, and therefore the size of the con-tribution gap. If pension reform is postponed by m years, equation (11) can again be used to calculate the constant contribution rate needed from year $t + m$ onwards to preserve sustainability of the pub-lic pension fund. The constant contribution rate with pension reform postponed by m years is given by

$$c_{t=m,n}^* = [(1 - \prod_{j=0}^{n} d_{t+j})b_{t-1} + \sum_{j=0}^{n} (\prod_{k=j+1}^{n} d_{t+k}) p_{t+j}$$

$$- \sum_{j=0}^{m-1} (\prod_{k=j+1}^{n} d_{t+k}) c_{t+j}]/\sum_{j=m}^{n} (\prod_{k=m+1}^{n} d_{t+k}). \qquad (14)$$

Pension Fund Balance Sheet

Given projections of fund revenue and expendi-ture between t and $t + n$, the financial position of the fund may be summarized by the pension fund bal-ance sheet. The pension fund balance sheet shows the initial net asset position and the present value of projected revenue of the fund on the asset side and the present value of pension expenditure on the lia-bility side.

The present value of pension expenditure in the balance sheet in turn can be broken down into three components: (1) the present value of pension pay-ments projected to accrue to present retirees between t and $t + n$; (2) the present value of pension payments projected to accrue to members of the present work-force based on their present work history; and (3) projected pension payments based on pension rights that accrue after 1995, reflecting both additional pen-sion rights accruing to the present workforce and new pension rights accruing to new labor force entrants.

The calculation of pension payments accruing to present retirees is based on assumptions about gen-der- and cohort-specific life expectancies. The cal-culation of the net pension liability accrued to the present workforce proceeds in two steps. First, for each cohort presently in the workforce the value of the pension in 1995 given the contribution history of the cohort is calculated. Second, based on assump-tions regarding life expectancies, for each cohort the present value of pension payments based on the first-step calculation is determined. The resulting values summed across all cohorts represents the pension liability accrued to the present workforce ("recognition bonds"). The pension liability due to the accumulation of new rights is calculated as the residual between the gross pension liability and the pension liabilities accrued to present retirees and the present workforce.

The calculation of the fiscal implications of a gradual transition to a fully funded system is based on the assumption that the first cohort paying into the fully funded system is aged 15–19 in the year 2000. As a consequence, none of the cohorts that pays into the fully funded system under the gradual transition scheme will retire over the projection pe-riod, and there will be no expenditure from the fully funded system. At the same time, the public pension fund will (approximately) be phased out over the projection period. Neglecting pension expenditure beyond 2050, the gradual transition case can be rep-resented as a "reshuffling" of liabilities and assets between the public pension system and the fully funded system. After consolidation of the two sys-tems, the net pension liability corresponds exactly to the net pension liability under present pension arrangements.

To calculate the fiscal implications of a sudden transition to a fully funded system, it is necessary to also keep track of the pension expenditure from the fully funded system. Under this case, all contribu-tions flow to the fully funded system. The expendi-ture flow from the fully funded system is determined in two steps. First, gender- and cohort-specific con-tributions are accumulated (with interest) up to the year of retirement of the cohort. Second, the accu-mulated gender- and cohort-specific funds are con-verted into an inflation-indexed annuity in the year of retirement (this requires making assumptions about life expectancies). For a given year, summing the annuity flows across cohorts gives the pension expenditure flow of the fully funded system, which can then be converted into a present value for 1995. The difference between the present value of expen-diture and contribution flows—for the period 1995–2050—to the fully funded system provides an estimate of the "net pension liability" of the fully funded system.

Other Data Sources

United States

Cohort- and gender-specific labor market data are taken from U.S. Department of Labor, *Employment and Earnings* (Washington, D.C.: various issues). Data on pension revenue and expenditure from U.S. Board of Trustees of the Federal Old-Age and Survivors Insurance and Disability Insurance Trust Funds, *1995 Annual Report* (Washington, D.C.: 1995) and Eugene C. Steuerle and Jon M. Bakija, *Retooling Social Security for the 21st Century Right and Wrong Approaches to Reform* (The Urban Institute Press, Washington, D.C.: 1994).

Japan

Cohort- and gender-specific labor force participation and unemployment rates are taken from *OECD Labour Force Statistics* (Paris: various issues). Data on cohort- and gender-specific wages are staff estimates. Data on pension revenue and expenditure from Shakai Hosho Kenkyujo, "The Cost of Social Security in Japan," *SDRI: Statistical Report,* No. 1 (Tokyo: 1990).

Germany

Cohort- and gender-specific labor market data and the data on the revenue and expenditure of the public pension system are taken from *Statistisches Jahrbuch für die Bundesrepublik Deutschland* (various issues). The data on the public pension system cover the wage and salary earners' pension insurance funds (*Rentenversicherung der Arbeiter und Angestellten*).

France

Cohort- and gender-specific labor force participation and unemployment rates are taken from INSEE, "Taux d'activité au sens du BIT par sexe et age quinquennal," *Serie Emploi-Revenus* (Paris: 1994). Cohort- and gender-specific wage data were provided by Direction de la Prévision, Ministère de l'Economie. Pension revenue and expenditure data originate from the *Livre Blanc Sur les Retraites,* Documentation Française, 1991.

Italy

Cohort- and gender-specific labor force participation and unemployment rates are taken from *OECD Labour Force Statistics* (Paris: various issues). Estimates of cohort- and gender-specific wages are staff estimates. Pension revenue and expenditure data originate from INSTAT, *Statistiche sui Trattamenti Pensionistici al 31 Dicembre 1992* (1994c); INSTAT, *Annuario Statistico Italiano* (1994a); and INSTAT, *Statistiche della Previdenza, della Sanita' e dell'Assistenza Sociale* (1994b).

United Kingdom

Cohort- and gender-specific labor force participation and unemployment rates are taken from *OECD Labour Force Statistics* (Paris: various issues). Estimates of cohort- and gender-specific wages are staff estimates. Data on pension revenue and expenditure are taken from *Government Actuary's Department, National Insurance Fund: Long Term Financial Estimates* (London: HMSO, 1990).

Canada

Cohort- and gender-specific labor force participation and unemployment rates are taken from *OECD Labour Force Statistics* (Paris: various issues). Cohort- and gender-specific wages from Beach and Slotsve, "Polarization of Earnings in the Canadian Labor Market," *in Stabilization, Growth and Distribution: Linkages in the Knowledge Era,* ed. by T. Courchene (Kingston, Ontario: 1994). Data on pension revenue and expenditure from Canada Pension Plan and Quebec Pension Plan, *Actuarial Report* (1992 and 1993).

Sweden

Cohort- and gender-specific labor force participation rates from *OECD Labour Force Statistics* (Paris: various issues). Cohort- and gender-specific unemployment and wage data from Riksförsälringsverket, *National Social Insurance Board Statistik Arsbok 1995* (Stockholm: 1995). Data on pension revenue and expenditure from Riksförsäkringsverket (1994) and Statistika Centralbyran, *Social Insurance Statistics* (Stockholm: various issues).

Appendix II   Bibliographic Notes

Social Security and Aging Populations

Since World War II, pension expenditures in industrial countries have risen sharply (as a percent of GDP), reflecting rising numbers of beneficiaries, an increase of the generosity of benefits, and the maturation of public pension schemes (OECD (1988a)). Since the early 1980s, the prospect of aging populations has widely been recognized and discussed as a key fiscal and macroeconomic problem, as detailed in studies by Heller, Hemming, and Kohnert (1986), OECD (1988b), Hagemann and Nicoletti (1989), Cutler and others (1990), Van den Noord and Herd (1993, 1994), and more recently World Bank (1994), Leibfritz and others (1995), and Masson and Mussa (1995).

Studies carried out in several countries have also identified demographic developments as the main threat to the financial sustainability of social security arrangements. See, for example, Board of Trustees (1995) for the United States; Noguchi (1992) for Japan; *PROGNOS-Gutachten* 1995 (1995) for Germany; *Livre Blanc sur les Retraites* (1991) for France; Government Actuary's Department (1990) for the United Kingdom; and Murphy and Smith (1992) for Canada.

Parametric Reform Approaches to Public Pension Reform

Various expenditure-reducing policy options applicable within a PAYG framework have been considered and several have been adopted in pension reforms recently enacted in various countries. A first group includes measures aimed at containing the growth in the number of beneficiaries: increasing the statutory retirement age, tightening eligibility criteria, and disincentives for early retirement. A second group includes measures aimed at reducing per capita benefits: assessment of past earnings over a longer period, partial uprating of assessed past earnings, reductions in accrual rates, and modifications to the indexation mechanisms. See Halter and Hemming (1987) and Van den Noord and Herd (1994) among others. Different pension indexation options are discussed by Hemming and Kay (1982) and Hills (1993).

In the United States, in 1983, a reform was enacted to change the structure of the old-age and disability insurance system. These included a shift from PAYG to partial funding, and a gradual increase in contribution rates and in the statutory retirement age. For details of past and present pension reform debates in the United States see Munnell (1977) and Steuerle and Bakija (1994). In Japan, far-reaching legislation was enacted in 1985 and again in 1994; changes included increases in contribution rates and in the legal retirement age, a reduction in the accrual rate from 1 to 0.75 percent, and indexation of benefits to net instead of gross wage growth. A detailed discussion of the issues raised by the 1994 reform can be found in Takayama (1995). In Germany, the 1992 Pension Reform Act introduced several measures to improve the long-term viability of the pension system: gradual increase in the statutory retirement age, reduced incentives for early retirement, indexation of benefits to net instead of gross wage growth, automatic increases in the contribution rates when expenditures are anticipated to exceed revenues and accumulated reserves are insufficient. See Deutsche Bundesbank (1995) for a summary of public pension reform issues and proposals in Germany. In the United Kingdom, the 1986 Social Security Act replaced the best 20 years' rule for benefit computation with an average lifetime earnings calculations, and reduced the replacement rate from 25 to 20 percent. The reform is analyzed in Creedy and Disney (1988) and the more recent debates in the United Kingdom are covered by Blake (1995). Pension reform debates in France and Italy are surveyed by Levy (1995) and Canziani and Demekas (1995), respectively.

In an influential contribution, Musgrave (1981) argued that PAYG systems are best viewed as arrangements for sharing demographic and economic risks between working and retired generations, giving rise to an implicit intergenerational contract.

Choice Between PAYG and Funded Systems

Debates on the choice between PAYG and fully funded or partially funded pension schemes involve a wide range of complex issues, such as distributional considerations and effects on labor markets, capital formation, private consumption, and saving. A classic contribution on the choice between a PAYG and a fully funded system is Aaron (1966), who shows that PAYG financing is superior to full funding, that is, provides a higher rate of return for each generation, if the sum of the rate of population growth and the rate of growth of real wages exceeds the market real rate of interest. Several studies, among them Keyfitz (1985), have tried to quantify the impact of aging on the rates of return on social security contributions of different cohorts under PAYG financing.

Diamond and Valdés-Prieto (1994) discuss Chile's privatization of its social security system and argue that the main benefits of the transition to a fully funded defined-contribution system in the case of Chile are the more consistent treatment of all workers, insulation of the pension system from politics, and development of domestic capital markets. Ribe (1994) reviews the fully funded public pension systems in Indonesia, Malaysia, and Singapore. He shows that, compared to a PAYG system, a fully funded system reduces economic distortions and encourages the development of financial markets; on the other hand, the fully funded systems considered in the paper appear to suffer from insufficient population coverage and variable and often inadequate replacement rates. In an early study, Kay (1983) discusses the concept of "notional funding" in the context of the social security system in the United Kingdom and concludes that actual accumulation of a pension fund is not required to reap the benefit of greater financial discipline on politicians attributed to fully funded pension systems.

General Equilibrium Analyses

The assessment of the long-run fiscal consequences of public pension reform in this study (and most of the other studies referenced in this bibliography) is based on given macroeconomic and demographic projections, and, as a consequence, neglects general equilibrium effects. Aaron, Bosworth, and Burtless (1989) examine the macroeconomic consequences of alternatives for financing social security in a traditional macroeconomic model. Masson and Tryon (1990) explore the macroeconomic effects of aging using the Fund's MULTIMOD model. Most of the recent analyses of public pension reform in a general equilibrium setting are based on the numerical overlapping-generations model pioneered by Auerbach and Kotlikoff (1987). For example, Auerbach, Kotlikoff, Hagemann, and Nicoletti (1989) use the Auerbach-Kotlikoff model to analyze the demographic transition and piecemeal pension reforms in Germany, Japan, Sweden, and the United States. They find that in a general-equilibrium framework the burden of financing a demographic transition is reduced because of taking into account the concomitant decrease in social expenditures targeted to the younger population, but is still very significant. An application of the Auerbach-Kotlikoff model to the issue of transition from a PAYG system to a fully funded system is Arrau and Schmidt-Hebbel (1993). They find that a debt-financed transition to a fully funded system has no effect on the economy while a tax-financed transition may have moderate positive effects, which are, however, reaped only by generations living in the distant future. Corsetti and Schmidt-Hebbel (1994) analyze the transition from PAYG to a fully funded system using an overlapping-generations model with endogenous growth and both a formal and an informal production sector. The transition eliminates the PAYG distortions in favor of the informal sector, and therefore leads to substantially higher long-term growth rates.

References

Aaron, Henry J. (1966), "The Social Insurance Paradox," *Canadian Journal of Economics and Political Science,* Vol. 32 (August), pp. 371–77.

———, Barry P. Bosworth, and Gary T. Burtless (1989), *Can America Afford to Grow Old? Paying for Social Security* (Washington: The Brookings Institution).

Arrau, Patricio, and Klaus Schmidt-Hebbel (1993), "Macroeconomic and Intergenerational Welfare Effects of a Transition from Pay-As-You-Go to Fully Funded Pension Systems" (unpublished; Washington: World Bank).

Auerbach, Alan J., and Laurence J. Kotlikoff (1987), *Dynamic Fiscal Policy* (Cambridge: Cambridge University Press).

———, Robert P. Hagemann, and Giuseppe Nicoletti (1989), "The Economic Dynamics of an Aging Population: The Case of Four OECD Countries," *OECD Economic Studies,* No. 12 (Spring), pp. 97–130.

Beach, Charles M., and George A. Slotsve (1994), "Polarization of Earnings in the Canadian Labor Market," in *Stabilization, Growth and Distribution: Linkages in the Knowledge Era,* ed. by Thomas J. Courchene (Kingston, Ontario), pp. 75–88.

Blake, David (1995), *Pension Schemes and Pension Funds in the United Kingdom* (Oxford: Clarendon Press).

Blanchard, Olivier J., and others (1990), "The Sustainability of Fiscal Policy: New Answers to an Old Question," *OECD Economic Studies,* No. 15 (Autumn), pp. 7–36.

Bos, Eduard, and others (1994), *World Population Projections 1994–95,* A World Bank Book (Baltimore and London: Johns Hopkins Press).

Canada Pension Plan (1993), *Actuarial Report for Canada* (Ottawa: Office of the Superintendent of Financial Institutions).

Canziani, Patrizia, and Dimitri G. Demekas (1995), "The Italian Public Pension System: Current Prospects and Reform Options," IMF Working Paper 95/33 (Washington: International Monetary Fund).

Corsetti, Giancarlo, and Klaus Schmidt-Hebbel (1994), "Pension Reform and Growth," (unpublished; Washington: World Bank).

Creedy, John, and Richard Disney (1988), "The New Pension Scheme in Britain," *Fiscal Studies,* Vol. 9 (May), pp. 57–71.

Cutler, David M., and others (1990), "An Aging Society: Opportunity or Challenge?", *Brookings Papers on Economic Activity,* No. 1, pp. 1–73.

Davis, E.P. (1993), "The Structure, Regulation and Performance of Pension Funds in Nine Industrial Countries," World Bank Working Paper No. 1229 (Washington: World Bank).

Deutsche Bundesbank (1995), "The Finances of the Statutory Pension Insurance Funds Since the Beginning of the Nineties," *Deutsche Bundesbank Monthly Report* (March), pp.17–31.

Diamond, Peter, and Salvador Valdés-Prieto (1994), "Social Security Reform," in *The Chilean Economy: Policy Lessons and Challenges,* ed. by Barry P. Bosworth, Rudiger Dornbusch, and Raúl Labán (Washington: The Brookings Institution), pp. 257–328.

Feldstein, Martin (1996), "The Missing Piece in Policy Analysis: Social Security Reform," *American Economic Review,* Vol. 86, No. 2 (May), pp. 1–14.

Government Actuary's Department (1990), *National Insurance Fund: Long Term Financial Estimates* (London: HMSO).

Gramlich, Edward M. (1996), "Different Approaches for Dealing with Social Security," *American Economic Review,* Vol. 86, No. 2 (May), pp. 358–62.

Hagemann, Robert P., and Giuseppe Nicoletti (1989), "Population Aging: Economic Effects and Some Policy Implications for Financing Public Pensions," *OECD Economic Studies,* No. 12 (Spring), pp. 51–96.

Halter, William A., and Richard Hemming (1987), "The Impact of Demographic Change on Social Security Financing," *IMF Staff Papers,* Vol. 34, No. 3, pp. 471–502.

Heller, Peter S., Richard Hemming, and Peter W. Kohnert (1986), *Aging and Social Expenditure in the Major Industrial Countries, 1980–2025,* IMF Occasional Paper 47 (Washington: International Monetary Fund).

Hemming, Richard, and John A. Kay (1982), "The Cost of the State Earnings Related Pension Scheme," *Economic Journal,* Vol. 92 (June), pp. 300–17.

Hills, John (1993), "The Future of Welfare: A Guide to the Debate" (London: Joseph Rowntree Foundation).

Holzmann, Robert (1995), "Pension Reform, Financial Market Development and Endogenous Growth: Preliminary Evidence From Chile" (unpublished; Washington: International Monetary Fund).

Homburg, Stefan (1990), "The Efficiency of Unfunded Pension Schemes," *Journal of Institutional and Theoretical Economics,* Vol. 146, No. 4, pp. 640–47.

Institut National de la Statistique et des Etudes Economiques (1994), "Taux d'activité au sens du BIT par sexe et age quinquennal," *Serie Emploi-Revenus* (Paris: INSEE).

Istituto Nationale Di Statistica (1994a), *Annuario Statistico Italiano* (Rome: INSTAT).

_____ (1994b), *Statistiche della Previdenza, della Sanita' e dell'Assistenza Sociale* (Rome: INSTAT).

_____ (1994c), *Statistiche sui Trattamenti Pensionistici al 31 Dicembre 1992* (Rome: INSTAT).

Kay, John A. (1983), "The Finance of Public Sector Pension Schemes," Bank of England Panel of Academic Consultants, *Panel Paper*, No. 20.

Kenkyujo, Shakai Hosho (1990), "The Cost of Social Security in Japan," *SDRI: Statistical Report*, No. 1 (Tokyo).

Keyfitz, Nathan (1985), "The Demographics of Unfunded Pensions," *European Journal of Population*, Vol. 1, pp. 5–30.

Kotlikoff, Laurence J. (1995), "Privatizing Social Security: How It Works and Why It Matters," NBER Working Paper No. 5330.

Kuné, Jan B., and others (1993), "The Hidden Liabilities of the Basic Pension Systems in the Member States," Center for European Policy Studies Working Paper (Brussels, November).

Leibfritz, Willi, Deborah Roseveare, Douglas Fore, and Eckhard Wurzel (1995), "Ageing Populations, Pension Systems and Government Budgets: How Do They Affect Savings?", OECD Economics Department Working Paper No. 156 (Paris: OECD).

Levy, Joaquim V. (1995), "Some Considerations Relevant to Prefunded Pensions in France," IMF Working Paper 95/64 (Washington: International Monetary Fund).

Livre Blanc (1991), *Livre Blanc sur les Retraites* (Paris: Documentation Française).

Masson, Paul R., and Ralph W. Tryon (1990), "Macroeconomic Effects of Population Aging in Industrial Countries," *IMF Staff Papers*, Vol. 37 (September), pp. 435–85.

Masson, Paul R., and Michael Mussa (1995), "Long-Term Tendencies in Budget Deficits and Debt," IMF Working Paper 95/128 (Washington: International Monetary Fund).

Munnell, Alicia H. (1977), *The Future of Social Security*, Brookings Studies in Social Economics (Washington: The Brookings Institution).

———, and C. Nicole Ernsberger (1990), "Foreign Experience with Public Pension Surpluses and National Saving," in *Social Security's Looming Surpluses: Prospects and Implications*, ed. by Carolyn L. Weaver (Washington: American Enterprise Institute), pp. 85–118.

Murphy, E.M., and G. Smith (1992), "Promoting the Debate on Population Issues: the Innovations of the Demographic Review," in "Changing Population Age and Structure, 1990–2015" (Geneva: United Nations Economic Commission for Europe and United Nations Population Fund, United Nations).

Musgrave, Richard A. (1981), "A Reappraisal of Social Security Financing," in: *Social Security Financing*, ed. by Felicity Skidmore (Cambridge, Massachusetts: MIT Press), pp. 89–127.

Noguchi, Yukio (1992), "Aging Population, Social Security, and Tax Reform," in: *The Political Economy of Tax Reform*, ed. by Takatoshi Ito and Anne O. Krueger (Chicago: University of Chicago Press), pp. 211–23.

Organization for Economic Cooperation and Development (1988a), *Reforming Public Pensions* (Paris: OECD).

———, (1988b), *Ageing Populations: The Social Policy Implications* (Paris: OECD).

———, (various issues) *OECD Labour Force Statistics* (Paris: OECD).

Quebec Pension Plan (1992), *Actuarial Report for Canada* (Ottawa: Office of the Superintendent of Financial Institutions).

Ribe, Frederick C. (1994), "Funded Social Security Systems: A Review of Issues in Four East Asian Countries," *Revista de Analisis Economico*, Vol. 9, No. 1 (June), pp. 169–82.

Riksförsäkringsverket (1994), *Social Insurance Statistics-Facts 1994* (Stockholm: National Social Insurance Board).

Statistika Centralbyran (various issues), *Statistik Arsbok* (Stockholm: Statistika Centralbyran).

Statistisches Bundesamt (various issues), *Statistisches Jahrbuch für die Bundesrepublik Deutschland* (Wiesbaden).

Steuerle, Eugene C., and Jon M. Bakija (1994), *Retooling Social Security for the 21st Century Right and Wrong Approaches to Reform* (Washington: Urban Institute Press).

Takayama, Noriguki (1995), "The 1994 Reform Bill for Public Pensions in Japan: Its Main Contents and Related Discussion," *International Social Security Review*, Vol. 48, No.1, pp. 45–65.

U.S. Board of Trustees of the Federal Old-Age and Survivors' Insurance and Disability Insurance Trust Funds (1995), *1995 Annual Report* (Washington, D.C.).

U.S. Department of Labor (various issues), *Employment and Earnings* (Washington, D.C.)

Van den Noord, Paul, and Richard Herd (1993), "Pension Liabilities in the Seven Major Economies," Economics Department Working Papers No. 142 (Paris: OECD).

_____ (1994), "Estimating Pension Liabilities: A Methodological Framework," *OECD Economic Studies*, No. 23 (Winter), pp. 131–66.

Verband Deutscher Rentenversicherungsträger (1995), *PROGNOS-Gutachten* (Frankfurt).

World Bank (1994), *Averting the Old Age Crisis* (Oxford: Oxford University Press).

Recent Occasional Papers of the International Monetary Fund

147. Aging Populations and Public Pension Schemes, by Sheetal K. Chand and Albert Jaeger, 1996

146. Thailand: The Road to Sustained Growth, by Kalpana Kochhar, Louis Dicks-Mireaux, Balazs Horvath, Mauro Mecagni, Erik Offerdal, and Jianping Zhou. 1996.

145. Exchange Rate Movements and Their Impact on Trade and Investment in the APEC Region, by Takatoshi Ito, Peter Isard, Steven Symansky, and Tamim Bayoumi. 1996.

144. National Bank of Poland: The Road to Indirect Instruments, by Piero Ugolini. 1996.

143. Adjustment for Growth: The African Experience, by Michael T. Hadjimichael, Michael Nowak, Robert Sharer, and Amor Tahari. 1996.

142. Quasi-Fiscal Operations of Public Financial Institutions, by G.A. Mackenzie and Peter Stella. 1996.

141. Monetary and Exchange System Reforms in China: An Experiment in Gradualism, by Hassanali Mehran, Marc Quintyn, Tom Nordman, and Bernard Laurens. 1996.

140. Government Reform in New Zealand, by Graham C. Scott. 1996.

139. Reinvigorating Growth in Developing Countries: Lessons from Adjustment Policies in Eight Economies, by David Goldsbrough, Sharmini Coorey, Louis Dicks-Mireaux, Balazs Horvath, Kalpana Kochhar, Mauro Mecagni, Erik Offerdal, and Jianping Zhou. 1996.

138. Aftermath of the CFA Franc Devaluation, by Jean A.P. Clément, with Johannes Mueller, Stéphane Cossé, and Jean Le Dem. 1996.

137. The Lao People's Democratic Republic: Systemic Transformation and Adjustment, edited by Ichiro Otani and Chi Do Pham. 1996.

136. Jordan: Strategy for Adjustment and Growth, edited by Edouard Maciejewski and Ahsan Mansur. 1996.

135. Vietnam: Transition to a Market Economy, by John R. Dodsworth, Erich Spitäller, Michael Braulke, Keon Hyok Lee, Kenneth Miranda, Christian Mulder, Hisanobu Shishido, and Krishna Srinivasan. 1996.

134. India: Economic Reform and Growth, by Ajai Chopra, Charles Collyns, Richard Hemming, and Karen Parker with Woosik Chu and Oliver Fratzscher. 1995.

133. Policy Experiences and Issues in the Baltics, Russia, and Other Countries of the Former Soviet Union, edited by Daniel A. Citrin and Ashok K. Lahiri. 1995.

132. Financial Fragilities in Latin America: The 1980s and 1990s, by Liliana Rojas-Suárez and Steven R. Weisbrod. 1995.

131. Capital Account Convertibility: Review of Experience and Implications for IMF Policies, by staff teams headed by Peter J. Quirk and Owen Evans. 1995.

130. Challenges to the Swedish Welfare State, by Desmond Lachman, Adam Bennett, John H. Green, Robert Hagemann, and Ramana Ramaswamy. 1995.

129. IMF Conditionality: Experience Under Stand-By and Extended Arrangements. Part II: Background Papers. Susan Schadler, Editor, with Adam Bennett, Maria Carkovic, Louis Dicks-Mireaux, Mauro Mecagni, James H.J. Morsink, and Miguel A. Savastano. 1995.

128. IMF Conditionality: Experience Under Stand-By and Extended Arrangements. Part I: Key Issues and Findings, by Susan Schadler, Adam Bennett, Maria Carkovic, Louis Dicks-Mireaux, Mauro Mecagni, James H.J. Morsink, and Miguel A. Savastano. 1995.

127. Road Maps of the Transition: The Baltics, the Czech Republic, Hungary, and Russia, by Biswajit Banerjee, Vincent Koen, Thomas Krueger, Mark S. Lutz, Michael Marrese, and Tapio O. Saavalainen. 1995.

126. The Adoption of Indirect Instruments of Monetary Policy, by a staff team headed by William E. Alexander, Tomás J.T. Baliño, and Charles Enoch. 1995.

125. United Germany: The First Five Years—Performance and Policy Issues, by Robert Corker, Robert A. Feldman, Karl Habermeier, Hari Vittas, and Tessa van der Willigen. 1995.

124. Saving Behavior and the Asset Price "Bubble" in Japan: Analytical Studies, edited by Ulrich Baumgartner and Guy Meredith. 1995.

123. Comprehensive Tax Reform: The Colombian Experience, edited by Parthasarathi Shome. 1995.

122. Capital Flows in the APEC Region, edited by Mohsin S. Khan and Carmen M. Reinhart. 1995.

121. Uganda: Adjustment with Growth, 1987–94, by Robert L. Sharer, Hema R. De Zoysa, and Calvin A. McDonald. 1995.

120. Economic Dislocation and Recovery in Lebanon, by Sena Eken, Paul Cashin, S. Nuri Erbas, Jose Martelino, and Adnan Mazarei. 1995.

119. Singapore: A Case Study in Rapid Development, edited by Kenneth Bercuson with a staff team comprising Robert G. Carling, Aasim M. Husain, Thomas Rumbaugh, and Rachel van Elkan. 1995.

118. Sub-Saharan Africa: Growth, Savings, and Investment, by Michael T. Hadjimichael, Dhaneshwar Ghura, Martin Mühleisen, Roger Nord, and E. Murat Uçer. 1995.

117. Resilience and Growth Through Sustained Adjustment: The Moroccan Experience, by Saleh M. Nsouli, Sena Eken, Klaus Enders, Van-Can Thai, Jörg Decressin, and Filippo Cartiglia, with Janet Bungay. 1995.

116. Improving the International Monetary System: Constraints and Possibilities, by Michael Mussa, Morris Goldstein, Peter B. Clark, Donald J. Mathieson, and Tamim Bayoumi. 1994.

115. Exchange Rates and Economic Fundamentals: A Framework for Analysis, by Peter B. Clark, Leonardo Bartolini, Tamim Bayoumi, and Steven Symansky. 1994.

114. Economic Reform in China: A New Phase, by Wanda Tseng, Hoe Ee Khor, Kalpana Kochhar, Dubravko Mihaljek, and David Burton. 1994.

113. Poland: The Path to a Market Economy, by Liam P. Ebrill, Ajai Chopra, Charalambos Christofides, Paul Mylonas, Inci Otker, and Gerd Schwartz. 1994.

112. The Behavior of Non-Oil Commodity Prices, by Eduardo Borensztein, Mohsin S. Khan, Carmen M. Reinhart, and Peter Wickham. 1994.

111. The Russian Federation in Transition: External Developments, by Benedicte Vibe Christensen. 1994.

110. Limiting Central Bank Credit to the Government: Theory and Practice, by Carlo Cottarelli. 1993.

109. The Path to Convertibility and Growth: The Tunisian Experience, by Saleh M. Nsouli, Sena Eken, Paul Duran, Gerwin Bell, and Zühtü Yücelik. 1993.

108. Recent Experiences with Surges in Capital Inflows, by Susan Schadler, Maria Carkovic, Adam Bennett, and Robert Kahn. 1993.

107. China at the Threshold of a Market Economy, by Michael W. Bell, Hoe Ee Khor, and Kalpana Kochhar with Jun Ma, Simon N'guiamba, and Rajiv Lall. 1993.

106. Economic Adjustment in Low-Income Countries: Experience Under the Enhanced Structural Adjustment Facility, by Susan Schadler, Franek Rozwadowski, Siddharth Tiwari, and David O. Robinson. 1993.

105. The Structure and Operation of the World Gold Market, by Gary O'Callaghan. 1993.

104. Price Liberalization in Russia: Behavior of Prices, Household Incomes, and Consumption During the First Year, by Vincent Koen and Steven Phillips. 1993.

103. Liberalization of the Capital Account: Experiences and Issues, by Donald J. Mathieson and Liliana Rojas-Suárez. 1993.

102. Financial Sector Reforms and Exchange Arrangements in Eastern Europe. Part I: Financial Markets and Intermediation, by Guillermo A. Calvo and Manmohan S. Kumar. Part II: Exchange Arrangements of Previously Centrally Planned Economies, by Eduardo Borensztein and Paul R. Masson. 1993.

101. Spain: Converging with the European Community, by Michel Galy, Gonzalo Pastor, and Thierry Pujol. 1993.

Note: For information on the title and availability of Occasional Papers not listed, please consult the IMF Publications Catalog or contact IMF Publication Services.